SPIRITUAL SELF -REALISATION

SPIRITUAL SELF -REALISATION

JAI NARAIN PAREEK

ARAVALI BOOKS INTERNATIONAL (P) LTD.
NEW DELHI - 110 020

ISBN 81-86880-55-0
First Edition : 1999

SPIRITUAL SELF - REALISATION
Price : Rs. 200/-

Publisher : Aravali Books International (P) Ltd.,
W-30, Okhla Industrial Area, Phase II, New Delhi-110 020
Phones : 6911417, 6841564, Fax : 011-6849782
E-mail : Aravali@nde.vsnl.net.in

Printer : Aravali Printer & Publishers (P) Ltd., New Delhi-110 020

Contents

Foreword

The Divine Rule shows no favours. The realisation that came to Sant Gyaneaswar, Sri Ramkrishna Paramhans, Swami Vivekanand, Sri Arvind, Swami Pramanand, and Many others may came to any person reaching that inner stage. There is no consideration of caste and society; of educated, trained and of great and small. No one believes in the invaluable treasure, with an ordinary person. Only a pure heart may tell it's value. Those who can do so, become and feel rich themselves. Therefore, in the second part of this book I have made a collection of the experiences and the thoughts of renowned saints and yogis, so that the new entrants may develop faith in them and in their Sadhna fearlessly and unabatedly.

Besides, the readers, may also give credence to the ordinary looking sadhaks, (aspirants) inspired by the Divine grace they have received.

The world famous book 'Yogi' Kathamrita' by Swami Yogaand Paramhansa refers about the thoughts of his guide Yukteshwar- Maharaj, thus:

"Do you desire the divine cheese but for you only? Had not the kind tradional spiritual guides delivered their knowledge to others willingly would any one have realised God? God honey and the institutions are hives. Both are inevitable."

While writing this book, thoughts like these have haunted my mind. The collected treasure of sadhana should not stagnate only at one place like the water of a pond rather, it should keep flowing universally for the benefit of the World like the sacred current of 'Bhagirathi'

I have no comments on the realisation of the realised ones because the readers can read and understand them by themselves. I have of course to say something about my newly initiated 'Sadhaks' who have opted the path of spiritual evoluation.

I have described the experiences of these Sadhaks only who have been in my personal touch, have been telling me about themselves and seeking my guidance.

I have personally read about such experiences in the scriptures, and religious books concerned. I have found them true after comparing these with those referred to in the scriptures. I myself have passed through this curse, have experienced and benefitted myself. Therefore, I have full belief in the experiences of these 'Sadhaks'.

These 'Sadhaks' enjoyed themselves such 'Sanskaras' as to enable them in starting their experience and relisation soon. They developed repidly and they dascribed them to me unhesitatingly for seeking my guidance. It is my fortune that God has entrusted me with the responsibility of guiding such 'Sadhaks'.

I do not favour the recitation of feelings and experiences before every one. The Shastras have for-bidden this. Immature 'Sadhaks' should not speak about them because such expression restrains their occurance. The feelings of pride etc. Over take the 'Sadhk'. Disbeliefs and dislikes cause grief to the heart. So, the expression of the *anubhutiya* is for-bidden. But there is no rule that they should never be revealed to anyone. It is improper to keep a complete veil on them. Time and circumstances necessitate even the closest secret to be revealed. The Geeta and the Ramayan disallow strongly their expression but at the sametime they also laud the efforts of the revealers. In the Geeta, Lord Krishna says:

"O, Arjuna, this secret should not be revealed to any impure person at any time. It should not be revealed also to any unfaithful or to a person who criticises me".

It may also mean that these secrets may be revealed to those who are faithful and devoted ones. Such a revealer is the best benefactor and the most dear to God. Tulsidas also says in Ramcharit Manas:

"This sacret opic was composed by Lord Siva and it was kept concealed in his heart in the absence of a proper person and occasion. He had narrated this to Parvati because she was the most apt listener yet, there are some persons before whom the sacret story should not be narrated. It should never be told to the obstinate and the wicked; who dislike to hear to it, who are greedy, arrogant, lustful and anti-brahmin, even if they may happen to be Kings. This Ram-katha shoued be gladly narrated to those who love the company of the good and the great.

I have extented my hand towards such sadhaks only. It seems to me that in the success of this work, the hearty assistance of the people and many other known and unknown 'Sidhas', Divine powers, has been of great value. The blessings of the Gods and the Godesses also inspired me to write this.

I feel that it is the need of time and the wish of saintly and divine powers that these examples should be affirmed through the following generation of 'Sadhaks'.

I bow heartily to these inspiring souls who have helped in the completion of this work. I extend my gratefulness to the fraternity of Sadhaks, who have encouraged me. Lastly I bow at the sacred feet of Swami Ramanandji, my gurudev, who is the basic source of this book.

He has ever bestowed his grace upon me. I am also indebted to the publishers and their Editor Shri H.C. Seth for bringing out this English Version for global circulation and reference by taking unusually great pains. My grateful thanks are due to Prof. P.S. Verma and Prof. S.P. Ruhela of Jamia Millia Islamia University for their kind exertions through the manuscripts and help in the publication of this English Version of my Hindi Book 'Adhyatmik Divya Anubhutiyan' which is also published by Aravali Books International (P) Ltd. Prof P.S Verma has reviewed the manuscripts Prepared by Acharya Raja Ram Misr 'Syamraj Who himself has written about the auttor He has also kindly done the proof readings.

Buddha smiled today for the second time and India became a Neclear weapons State overnight. May the grace of 'Sidhas help usher an are of peace in this region and the World, the neclear threats not withstandings.

Jai Narayan Pareek
Sadhna Dham, Kankhal

About the Author

(Jai Narain Pareek - A prominent Sadhak and his Sadhana)

Farrukhabad, known as small Kashi in the religious circles, was given its present name about became two hundred years ago only. But it famous became for its ancient spiritual attainments. In modern times, many great saints made this soil sacred with the touch of their feet and many of them celebrated their births here. Many renowned saints like Swami Brahmanand, Swami Swarupanand, Uria baba, hari Baba, Swami Ram-Dev and Swami Ramanand etc. made their place of worship here. Along with them many house-holders like Shyam Sunder Gujarati, Shital Devi Shukla etc. earned a great respect for their devotion and self realisation. In the living Sadhaks, the name of Pt. Jainarayan Pareek is the foremost. He along with many others has served the Sadhak community by guiding and inspiring them with his devotion and spiritual behaviour.

Pareekji, 83 now, is a very respectable figure of the city, moving about pleasantly and radiating the bliss of his nature, behaviour innocence, simplicity and joyhood, those close to him, feel his power and influence, acquired by him by his long Sadhana and study. Though he is a permanent resident of this place, but has spent most of his time outside, during the course of his Sadhana or service as a teacher. At present he spends most of his time at Swami Ramanand, Sadhana Dham, kanakhal, Haridwar, U.P. editing the magazine Sadhana, holding spiritual camps and making communication with enlightened persons. He is always busy building and inspiring new aspirants where-ever he is. He is still very zealous. He is an idol of kind speech and behaviour.

I am proud and feel augmented in being given this opportunity of introducing him to readers of this wonderful work. I have been in his contact since 1940 or so. He was a friend of my father and that time was very much interested, and acting in literary, social or spiritual pursuits. The image of those times is just the evolved figure of the present matured personality. But he is still young with black hair fine teath and intact eyesight. He can walk on foot for miles suppressing feeling of hunger and thirst like a purn Yogi. He is very liberal, perfectly calm and happy, completely detached but always feeling and sharing the adversities of his followers, friends and family. He has wonderful memory and can recite and quote verses and passages of incredible length, without any effort or strain. What a yogi becomes after Sadhana, may be verified from his living and behaviour. It is really very delightful to express something about him.

The forefathers of Pareekji came to Farrukhabad from Rajasthan a century ago and settled here. He was born in 1914. He is like a Yogi, who assumes birth to complete his yogihood. His inclination towards spiritual life became visible since his birth. The ambition in his early life was to prepare himself as a preacher and in order to achieve that end he deserted his house in his youth and reached Varanasi. For sometime he studied sanskrit and philosophy at the feet of Darshan Kesari Gopal Shastri of Kashi Vidyapith. But he had to give up that at the insistence of his parents.

HIS EDUCATION AND TEACHING PROFESSION

Pareekji Passed Vernacular Middle Examination in 1933 and took his teacher training at Allahabad Normal School for two years. He started his career as a teacher in 1940 and taught at Shamli Middle School, Bhalepur and Bhartiya Pathshala Inter College for Sometime. In 1952, he proceeded to Inter College Dev Prayag (Garhwal) with a view of having favourable atmosphere for his Sadhna and remained there for twenty years. He retired in 1978 from Panher Inter College, Etawah. He passed Sahitya Ratna and B.A, also during the course of his service. At present he enjoys himself of his pension and devoting his time in preaching and Sadhana freely. He worked for sometime at Geeta Press Gorakhpur and at Rishikal Churu also. His education, his career as a teacher, and his spiritual evoluation took place simultaneously. His mission of life now is completely to awaken and inspire the young generation to tread the path of knowledge and realisation. The present book is also an humble effort in that direction because he has assured by quoting the example of renowned sadhaks of late, as well as of the new Young sadhaks associated with him.

THE SPIRITUAL AWAKENING

The spiritual march of Pareekji started with his association with Shri Gopal Shastri of Varanasi. During those very days a Yagna, was to take place for six months based on a Doha of Tulsidas under the efforts of Prabhu Dutta Brahmachari of Jhansi. Pareekji Jointed the yagna and started the Jap of "Hare Krishna Here Krishna, Krishna Krishna, Here Hare." He listened the Bhagwati katha, took part in the 'Jap', and used to take fruits and milk for food and observed silence (Maun). This sadhana paved his future path. Even when he was a student of Vernacular Middle School he did Sandhya Gaytri Jap and read Gita. Dhyan Yog had also started. He started losing the body presence. Once the picture of Krishna, printed on the book of Gita became alive. Wherever he saw, he found the glimpse of Lord Krishna.

Pareekji, remained in the association of Jaidyal Goenka also for sometime. He used to note down the speeches of Goenka with his permission. He also wrote down the letters dictated by him. This association of Jaidayal Goenka and Hanuman Prasad Podder, helped him in furthering his associations and acquaintances. The initiation into the integral yog of Pareekji started with the help of Shri Trijugi Dayal Dixit, his friend and a resident of village Pipar goan. Swami Yogananda used to visit Dixit Ji, Pareekji had an opportunity to have ample communication with him. Once the association with him lasted for a month in a garden. His 'Sadhana' deepened from 1943 when he had his first meeting with Swami Ramananda in Farrukhabad. The Credit of this meeting goes to his close friend Babu Ram Misra. Whenever Swamiji came to Farrukhabad, Pareek Ji never missed to join the Satsangas and the meditations of Swamiji. He participated in the Sadhna camp of Swamiji held at Tari near Kanpur. After his initiation, from 1949 to 1950, he had a close contact with Swamiji and took part in all his camps held during this period at Syahi Devi (Almora). He had the 'Shakti Pat' in the camp at Syahi Devi and his yogic interactions started since then. The experiences of those days opened the doors of inside automatically. He remained grateful to Swamiji for his grace and he got an appointment as a teacher in a School at Dev Prayag with his efforts. He Participated in the last camp of Swamiji in Allahabad. Even today Pareekji is under the greatest influence of Swami Ramanand. His Sadhna has developed on the system initiated by Swami Ramananda. After the demise of Swami Ramananda, Pareekji had a contact with Swami Satyananda, the guide of Swami Ramananda. He enjoyed himself the love and blessings of Swami Satyanand Ji for a long time.

The twenty years of Sadhana spent at Devprayag may be called the golden period of the Sadhana of Pareekji while living here he had a long communication with yogies, saints, priests and other kinds of spiritual people. His Sadhna grew intenser day be day. He used to spend most of his time in going to remote places alone and to make a quest for the divine spirit manifested through the trees, the stones, the animals and the beasts. He felt the presence of the divine everywhere and in everything. This type of Sadhana purified his heart and confirmed the feeling of oneness in him. During this very period, he had meetings with the famous writer of 'Maha Yog Vigyan, Swami Yoganand Thirth', Swami Purushottamanand ji of Vasisth Gufa of (Garhwal), Sacchababa of.'Swami Kulananda ji of Arial of Allahabad, Swami Gayatri Baba, the writer of 'Sidha Yoga and the deciple of Swami Purushattma Nanda, and many other saints and Sages of that time. Many a time during the school holidays, he used to mediate at the top of some hill from morning to evening. These tops and peaks exhibited the whole grandeur of the great Himalayas. This love warship and mediation influenced his life deeply.

From the context and the associations and the practice, it becomes evident that Pareekji has been blessed with some spiritual realization also. He has an experience of the awakening and energising the divine power. It has been his practice to note down his experiences incurred during the meditation. He is a voracious speaker and a writer both. He does so to enable the new sadhaks to know and feel the process of sadhana properly. He has a number of note books containing his own experiences along with the experiences of the Sadhaks initiated or directed by him. It is no use saying that a number of Sadhaks have been inspired and guided by him the experiences of whom the readers will go throw in this book.

His speech is full of sweetness, simplicity and clarity. It is the result of his Sadhana. He has retained a wonderful memory and can recite and quote amply through the 'Shastras', the Ramayan and the other books read by him. He has full command over Urdu and Sanskrit. He has achieved a position now that he can energise others. He never speaks about his powers nor does he ever pose to be of any high order. He is very humble and is beyond ordinary praise or reproach, only his followers may have a guess and a feel of his powers. Those who revere him and have faith in him, may benefit themselves. Undoubtedly, Shri Pareekji is a symbol of the Sadhak who lives a transformed life. Pareekji in the true sense is a combination of a Gyani, a bhakt and Yogi. He is a preacher as well as the one who follows what one preaches. He has nothing like 'Sampradayik Duragrah'. His only wish is that the people should become spiritual and holy by following any system that suits them. He has made a deep study of the systems and the realizations of great Sidha Yogies like Ram Krishna Paramhans, Shri Arvind, Swami Vivekananda, Swami Satya Nanda and Swami Ram nanda extra. He has also kept an account of the progress of the Sadhaks, practising under his guidance. The purpose of this book is certainly to make an analysis of the Sadhana of the new entrants for the benefit of others, who are yet to tread that path. He hopes that the study of this book shall inspire the new generation in believing in the experiences of the old and the new Sadhaks. They will march on this path having full and firm faith. Many Sadhaks are progressing under his inspiration and guidance. The author of these lines feels immensely proud in writing something about Pareekji, who is to him a sincere friend, and inspirer and a guide as well. My long association with him has proved as a great asset to me in my own humble journey of life of knowledge and of spirituality. May God bless him with a prolonged life to provide him further opportunity for spreading the light of spirituality.

This English Version of his Hindi book '*ANUBUTIYON KE PATH PAR*' is prepared by me. I am however thankful to Professor P.S. Verma for editing & proof reading of this edition in english. I also appreciate for all the cooperation extended by the publisher M/s Aravali Books International (P) Ltd. in bringing out this publication.

Prof. Raja Ram Misra 'Shyam Raj'
Retd, Head of English Deptt, Kumayun University
Acharya 'Shyam Dhyan Dendra
3/5, Haribhagat Street
Farrukhabad (U.P)

Swami Ramanand Ji

Birth and Childhood — Swami Ramanand Ji, an ideal of pure love, selfless service and constant advancement, was born on 16th December, 1916 in a Punjabi Khatri family in Lalitpur near Jhansi, where his father, Dr. Sain Das carried his trade. He was named 'Shishupal' at his birth. His childhood passed here peacefully. At the age of two and a half, he lost his mother and was brought up by his mother like Sister-in-laws (Bhabhi). His additional place of residence was Bairownwall, a village near Tarantaran in Amritser District.

Education — He was a brilliant scholar since the start. He always stood first and never second. As a result of this, he enjoyed himself of scholarship from class V upto M.A. Being a brilliant scholar, he remained an object of love and favour of his class-mates and of his teachers. When he reached higher classes, he started reading Gandhian literature. His soul consciousness was awakened. He felt interested in Huth Yoga and started exercises like Asnas and Pranayam etc.

He top-ped the list of students of Punbaj in the Intermediate Examination. He studied the literature of Swami Vivekanand and Shri Arvindo. His inclianation increased towards the study of philosophy and spiritualism. He passed B.A. With English, Sanskrit and Philosophy. In the meantime, he developed taste for Yog. His inner door of experiences opened wide and fast. He felt that God had accepted him. He felt the need of a spiritual guide which resulted in his association with Swami Satyanandji. His attitudes towards life changed completely. The struggle between heart and mind culminated in the victory of the heart. The pure love, unique kindness and true affection of Swami Satyanandji sublimated his heart. The two became intimate more and more. He stood first in B.A. also. He took to the study of M.A., first in philosophy then in English literature. He took the degree of Shastri in Sanskrit also after that.

Leaving the home

One day, he had an internal call and turmoil. He told the members of his family that after one month he would give himself completely to God. The members of his family wanted to keep him with them but they could do nothing. They insisted, shed tears but all in vain. At last, the parting day arrived. The members of the family wept and cried. He needed the blessings and the permission of Swami Satyanandji. Swami Satyanand tried to dissuade him from his resolve but God had destined otherwise. Lastly, a young man of twenty five deserted the family sad and weeping and went away to make the world of his own.

A new life started and a new Sadhana began, the Sadhana of universal love. His experiences of previous life got expressed through his speeches like the smell of the buds radiating around after the opening of the buds. His fame also spread all around.

He made continuous service the object of his life. He started giving messages and spreading his light in every direction a lean and thin body but full of light and energy. He gave a call to follow him. He assured them to lead them to the fountain of Ramamrit, to the kingdom of eternity where all griefs end, and unlimited happiness prevails.

Towards the Himalayas

After leaving home, he procceeded towards the Himalayas. A small hut in a mountain village near Digouli (Almora) became his abode. He penanced there lonely. He recited the nectar of Shri Mad-Bhawat for six months there. He recited Ramayan also with such intensity that the listeners became full of ecstasy.

Guru-Worship

He remembered his guru on every Guru Poornima enthusiastically and faithfully and offered his worship to him with folded hands. In 1941 Swami Satyanandji came to Nainital and sent a message for him to see him. He journeyed from Digowli to Nainital on foot. Swami Satyanandji came to receive him himself leaving his Assan and embrassed him. The union of the two appeared like the travelling by bus towards Some shwer, he was God in person and was also blessed him to gain his goal of life soon.

Compassion

He felt that God had accepted him as his instrument. He felt a cry rising within him which said, "Mother, how full of unhappiness this world is" Mother, how could you bear with all this but yes, your power and Leala is beyond apprehention, so is thy compassion and grace! O Mother! have mercy so that the tears of the world may dry up! turn into the cradle of your Divine love.

Renunciation and Detachment

Swamiji never kept money with him. He never in his life made any Aashram or place of residence for him. The devotees wished to offer him the ready-built Aashram and were also ready to contribute millions of Rupees, but he never obliged them for that.

Into the Planes

He blessed the soil of Fatehgar (Farrukhabad) with his feet by coming here on 15th November, 1941 from Digouli with one of his devotee Shri Vanshidhar Joshi. He preached among the devotees at many places. The writer had also an occasion to listen to him. He became an annual visiter to Farrukhabad and stayed with Shri Bhagwati Parsad, a lawyer and held Satsangas, Pravachanas, Japas and Meditations during those visits. I also participated in those activities. Once, he went to Shrangi Rampur along with his devotees for having a dip in the holy Ganga. From there, he went to Kamalganr to visit and to pay homage to Swami Sacchidanand. Swami Sacchidanand embraced him with joy. They took evening walks daily with the group of devotees. The Sadhana family increased by and by. Swami Ramanandji started going to every village to every city in order to spread the message of Ram Nam.

Works

Swami Ji wrote a number of books in Hindi and English. Out of them Adhyatmic Vikas, Adhyatmic Sadhana Part-I and II, Geeta Vimersh, kailash Durshan and Jeevan Rahasya are very popular. He offered solutions to the spiritual and worldy problems of his devlotees by writing and answering thousands of letters. A Collection of which has been published under the title 'Patra Piyush'.

Service to Humanit

He was always eager to persuade the people on to the path of divinity. The Sadhaks put before him unhesitatingly all their internal and external problems and got solutions there-off. He cured the patients by going to them for miles and miles. He helped with money the Sadhaks that were under hardship. Sometimes, he became so compassionate that he got transferred into himself the physical ailments of others. He made others rid of diseases by suffering himself.

His System of Sadhana

In his system of Sadhana, the inner call, intensity, faith, love, the feeling of service and Nam Jap are the important elements. He said that the light is God. Its follow up may make the descent of conscious energy very easy. The name and the Named one (Naami) are one. The Named one pervades the Name. The Worship of the Name becomes the worship of the Naami 'Nam-Jap' is the best means of spiritual evolution.

Yatras (Visits)

He visited most of the famous shrines in India i.e. Mathura, Vrindavan, Ayodhaya, Kashi, Puri, navdeep, Kamakhya, Rameshwer, Badri Nath and Kailash Mansarover. He visited Ashramas of many renowned saints as well.

The Parting :

He kept ailing since the Allahabad Camp in January, 1952. He was treated in Ramkrishna Mission Hospital, Kankhal. Since death is inevitable and none can change the fate, framed by the Creator, this grand personality also ascended to its heavenly abode on 15th April, 1952.

Post Script:

Swami Ramanand has no more his physical frame but his spirit is still active. The devotees of Swami Ramanand have built a Sadhana Dham in his name at Kankhal in Haridwar. His practice of holding camps twice a year is still continuing and the Sadhaks that surrender themselves faithfully receive the blessings of Swami Ramanand Ji even today. Sometimes the blessed Sadhaks seem to receive Guru Deeksha of Ram Nam through the pious portrait of Swami ji placed in the hall of Sadhana Dham. His followers spread over the country are always busy in spreading his message of Ram Nam. The writer is one of such humble followers of the great Saint Swami Ramanand. We bow to him reverently again and again.

Part One
SADHANA KHAND

The Purpose of Sadhana

Before one starts treading the path of Sadhana its aim and purpose should be properly understood. Of course, the aim reveals itself as the sadhak proceeds in his practice but he should try to learn and know what is possible.

It is nature's law that the part always tries to revenite with the whole and it rests only when it is finally united with that. It is like the same as the piece of a stone, hurled upwards, goes upto a certain hight but comes down soon on the earth on account of the gravitational pull. The piece rests only when it comes to the earth.

The sun Vapourises water from the ocean, forms clouds of it and makes it rain to drain into the streets, on to the Occan again to be the same. Fire is a form of sun and when it burns, the flames always aspire towards the Sun. The air filled in a ballon always struggles to unite with the air outside. The sky is an empty void but when a certain part of it is separated, it endeavors to be the whole again. Likewise the human soul which has been separated from God, the Divine rather, hankers for its reunion with that, knowingly or unknowingly. Thus, the purpose of man's life is to regain Godhood anyhow. This consumation of attaining God, may be termed liberation or emancipation from the pain of birth and death or anything. It is all the union of the individual should with the cosmic soul. Swami Ramanand said "that God, the supreme power is always at the back of the Sadhak. It is very near and very far both. TAT DURE, TADANTIKE."

A thing placed within the house, without knowledge, is very far but it is very near with its knowledge. Similarly God may be far away to the ignorant and very near to the knowers. In the absence of the faith in the knowledge of the existence of God, within one's heart – He would certainly be far off. Therefore the search has to be made within lest it may go Vain. Nanak has said:–

"Why search Him, in the forest?
He lives within you.
Like the fragrance of the flower
Like the reflection in the mirror

Appears He, with His full view.

That God is within. That conscious energy sparkles in the heart. Ignorantly the search is made outside. Reverse the process and you shall get the proof. The realisation takes place inside.

Hanuman, goes in search of Sita, the world mother. The Yogini Swayam Prabha advises him and says, ''If you wish to find Sita, close your eyes, divert your Vrittis inside, give up the worldly attachments and enter into the 'VIVAR'. Waste not your time in sitting here. Proceed further.'' This advice is symbolic because it refers to the yogic system of attaining the goal. She further says, ''Have full faith in your mission and surety in achievement. Cast off all regrets else they will weaken you. Inferiority will assail you.''

The clues given by tapaswani Swayam Prabha are vital to every sadhak. The goal can not be achieved without them. Hanuman followed them and won the object. Truely, the goal can be gained only by thinking and persuing persistently. But how these can be done? Through some form or figure? All the forms are his. He permeates them all. He is consciousness supreme, the source of all. Ponder deeply, meditate and feel yourself complete 'He'.

Gurudeva, has written:

''We are neither body, nor breath, nor mind, nor wit, chitta or Ahankar, we are beyond them. Our existence owes His, in every limb of body. One, who has realised his own powers, is a true form of Bhagwati Satta-conscious energy. ''Reaching oneself, means reaching God. Without this, all knowledge is a fraud.''

This kind of realisation is a possibility. True faith in the inner existence of God, is the initial stage and step of realisation.

God is one but the resides in all hearts like the sun, which is one, reflects into many waters through its says. Electricity is one but it lightens innunberable bulbs. The speaker on the T.V. is one but he is seen speaking different places. Likewise God Can enshrine every heart and We may realise it as well. The deeper me go, the worldly bonds fade and shatter. Though God is above the play of Gunas, He pranks in then. All the seen is the manifestation of His. He assumes the sense form, the devotee likes to see Him in side him. In the Gita, Lord Krishna says:–

''As one prays to me, so I appear to him'' Swami Ramanand also asserts:–

''The greatest proof of this is the realisation. Call Him and He shall answers surely. Those who call Haim, get a response. Those who advanced towards Him, received a sure advancement from Him. The biographies of the saints and sages are the proofs of this so, this call for him is one of the fundamentals of Yog.

Some realise through a sound and some through colours. A sadhak can experience the reality through mysterions working of that power. The experiences differ because of different levels and stages of consciousness of the devotee.

The goal of Sadhana is to attain total consciousness by evolving intensively. The Divine consciousness may descend upon through its own grace on the individual, the flow being made easy by the practice of INTEGRAL YOG.

Integral Yog and what it means (Sadhan)

A long long journey has to be performed for the final achievement. The path is not simple and smooth for the sadhak to tread upon easily. There are deep dales and hills to obstruct the journey. The gardness that seem pleasant in the beginning become hazardous. Sometimes the aspirant jumps to the top and the other moment is hurled into the pit of hopelessness on being misdirected by the mad imagination. Only the determined ones go on like HANUMAN fearlessly and reach their goal with the help of the guide and the guru.

Tulsidas, in the beginning of Ram Charit Manas, prays to Lord SHIVA and BHAWANI, in the forms of faith and reverence. He declares that no one can realise God, in the absence of these two elements. Swami Ramanand also writes:–

''The simple belief takes place in mind. The dome formed out of logic, shatters by logic itself. The wit plays this game daily-creating and destroying. The beliefs of only the firm minds stay and those of the infirm dissolve.''

The Geeta, describes the traits of a firm mind. ''The one who does not grieve in pan desires no happiness and is free form all kinds of attachment, envy, fear or anger, is the firm minded sage.''

The origin of belief takes place in the field of intelligence and it's effect is limited to it. But a strong belief affects the heart as well and fills it with envy and lust. This belief, when purified and mixed with Samadhi Chetna, transcends the greater hights and towards the consumtion.

FAITH

Faith is far above belief. It has its' origin in the super consciousness. In overwhelms both mind and heart. Faith consists of throught and feeling both; it is nearer to heart than to mind. Faith resides in soul and mere logic can not create it. Besides belief, the two other feelings of Love and reverence are there. Where they are belief automatically comes. True faith confirms the nearness to God. Faith is the foundation of Integral Yog. In the absence of faith, no achievement is possible. Sans faith, Integral Yog is lifeless. Faith and Only faith, leads the Sadhak to the goal and enables him to transcend the many fold fields of ignorance and pain. In the field of realisation, faith is an invaluable asset. A Sadhak has to have firm faith in the Divine Power. Surrender to it, is only possible with faith. The urge of the sadhak shall grow Strong and serious with faith. It will secure a response from the conscious energy. The call, within becomes a passport to the sadhak in the spiritual journey. All efforts are useless in its absence.

Communion (SATSANG)

The communion with the pious and the realised ones, helps in arousing the call and making it firm. It is the greatest means of achievement. The awakened soul, inspires and awakens others. The greater the communion, the greater the benefit. Lord Shanker enumerates the advantages of communions and says,

"A man becomes detached through satsang. He feels free from desires and lives a liberated life. With the dissolution of the desires, the mind becomes pure and peaceful leading to the final reunion or Moksha." Tulsidas adds:–

God realisation in not possible without Satsang. The grace of Ram, God, is not possible without grace by Himself; the individual soul can not attain peace without His Grace."

Selfstudy (Swadhyay)

Self study helps a lot. The stories of the experiences and the realisations of the sages and the yogis, always inspire the aspirant and encourage him to proceed in his devotion. The biography of Sri Ramkrishna Paramhances is a wonderful example.

Contemplation (Manan)

The third aid to spiritual evolution is contemplation. The study sould be deep lest every thing should over flow and go waste. If it is not well contemplated and digested and assimilated, only a momentry change shall occur and reversion shall take place soon.

Prayer

The fourth means is prayer. Pray to God to bestow you with a benign urge. It should be so strong as to make all the efforts of the world vain in altering it. The power of prayer is unlimited and invaluable.

Will Power

The highest power of the soul is will. The intellect, heart, Pran, and body all act under it. The will power affects and inspires them. The sadhak will have to deeply resolve to develop faith, the resolve emanating from the soul level. It should be maintained as it will hasten the fulfilment.

We have varied relationships with God, those of master-servant, father-son, guide and disciple, mother-son, lover-beloved, husbandwife and others that can be easily developed. The relationship may be developed according to ones desire and need. If one desired a form or a faith, he can rely on it gladly. All the means needed to develop faith, may be freely increased.

Abhipsa

A pious and persistent wish for the union with God, is called abhipsa. It germinates out of faith, like the sapling out of the seed. There is difference between faith and blind faith. Blind faith leads to suffering but noble faith helps in the evolution. A benign call for the union, is abhipsa, the strongest desire of the heart'.

As the stream is an imperative need for the engine, as the horse to drive the cart, fire for cooking food; in the same way Abhipsa is also a motivation for worship. All other means like study and contemplation singing hyms etc. are vain unless there is Abhipsa. Abhipsa open higher channels of Sadhana. The stronger the abhipsa, the easier and earlier the realisation. Therefore, every sadhak sould full him with this abhipsa.

Contentment and Gratitude

The sadhak should never be afraid of the farness of the journey of Sadhana. He sould never feel disheaterved. Everything shall occur slowly. The disenchantment will cause ficuleness and it would lead to doubts and disbeliefs.

Proper Attitude

A proper attitude to sadhana is needed and thus attitude can be formed by watching the results objectively. There should not be any kind of haste or hurry. Even a bit of change should be a cause of contentment. It is a sure sign of Mother's grace. A feeling of gratitude for that should be shown. The expression of gratitude helps in the process of evoluation.

Feeling contented does not mean the slackness in the efforts. It is simply a sign of satwaguna and not of Tamoguna. On the other hand, discontentment is Rajoguna which hampers the practice. So, contentment develops gratifulness and gratefulness develops faith. Faith is the most valuable thing in the fields of spiritual evoluation. It confirms sadhana.

Receptivity

A Sadhak requires great receptive power bestowed upon him by the grace of Mother. If the power descends upon him, and he is incapable of absorving it, no change shall occur in him. The light of the sun, the force of the wind can not react if the doors and the windows are shut. The consciousness starts working atonce, if it finds the field open. The receptive power of the sadhak depends on his faith for the Mother. The greater the faith, the greater the receptivity. The grand garden of God, lacks nothing. But if the satchel is small or shut, where will that flowery grace consist in. Nothing will materialise. A sadhak will have to extend and expand his vessel to have the grace. Some one has said :–

"Only the ignorant statisfies himself with a few buds. There is no limit to the grace of Almighty."

Therefore one has to be receptive enough. There is nothing to fear or falter. The receptivity will increase automatically in the course of worship and together grace of Divine Mother.

Self-Surrender

Real sadhana begins with self-surrender and cousumates also with it. Without self-surrender. The superconsciousness can not operate. The divine feelings do not develop without surrender. The union of the sadhak and God, takes place only when there is unconditional surrender. Belief, faith, urge, and capability are the beginnings only. Self surrender means consecrating all actions for Him only. The self surrender may, of course, may be of different intents and purposes also. Therefore the spiritual goal must be its basis.

Means of Integral Yog

The sadhak has to make a total surrender faithfully, lovingly and gratefully and not fearfully or favouredly. It must be the outcome of the urge intense like that of MEERABHAI who said,

"Oh, my mate of life and death
without you, Vain is my birth and breath
for Mights and days, I wail and, moan
In the hope of your face and form being shown.

This kind of Yearning is the secret of self-surrender. Self surrender, may always he superior to external, provided it is inspired by the heart.

The surrender offers an opportunity to the Divine Mother to scatter her grace on the sadhak. The great power can not descend and react unless total and unconditional surrender is made.

It is our egoness to say that we shall do. The consumation in sadhana is never passible without the elimination of ego. However, self sacrifice or surrender does not mean eliminating the body or life. Sacrifice is an adoration to self, the elimination of the feeling of doer ship. The fulfilment of manhood, the attainment of God hood is possible through integral Yog.

Our Sadhana Path

The Sadhan-path on which me tread, has been named Integral Yog' (Antar Yog) by gurudeva. It is called the Descending Path. The common definition of this is :

"The Integral Yog is the close union of the sadhak, with the loving creatoress world rather, the Super Power, in the Cave of the soul which is silent and secluded and whole".

The Super Power whom gurudev Swami Ramanand Calls Mother is omnipresent. It pervades the very atoms. There is no thing or place, where it is not formed. All the beings and the substances are her manifestation only. Shruti says :–

"The nectar like Brahma is before and behind, in the north and in the south; It is above and under. The whole world is nothing but Brahma,"

Another mantra describes :–

"He that is the tiniest and the mightiest, is conclaved in the heart cave. The one who comes to realises the resolveless God and His grandeur, with His grace, becomes griefless and achieves God. Who is bliss itself." The Upanishad Clarifies further :

"That One God, is hidden in all beings, is onmi-present and the life of all beings. He is the source, of all, seer, all conscious, the purest and above the Gunas. Alone He is the Controller of all insentient. He transforms the Nature-Seed into various forms. The firms and faithful realise that power and only they enjoy themselves of his bliss."

Through the Shastra, through the communion of the saints or through personal experience, when one comes to know of God and the purpose of life of attaining Him, the question arises as how to realise Him? The means through which how to realise HIm? the means through which God realisation is passible, are called SADHANA.

The saints and the sages have worshipped Him have realised Him, have described those means. The means differ but the aim is one Gurudev says :

"The aim of our sadhana is to evolve the self consciousness to the level of super-consciousness. We have seen that this can be possible only by the descendence of conscions-energy. This flow can be speeded up through the INTEGRAL Yog. We can invoke the Super Power to interact

Swiftly and we can proceed to self sacrifice through the same process. By complete surrender to that we may pray for Help and guidance.'' Gurudev has described the system, preached to us, through a letter dated 28-4-48 written from Digoli (Almora) to an aspirant:

''The descent of energy is possible even during the first vision in our system. But no resolve is made for special affection because the purpose of sadhana is to teach the means comprehensively, to enable the aspirant for the realisation, depending on him for the fulfilment of the mission. In our system also, the descent of energy is done with the name Power, by the guru the quality however, depending on the deserings of the sadhak. Some have instant interaction and in some the process is very slow. It all happens according to the individuals internal position. The Name is enlivened; the seed is sown. The developing worship and practice help in the growth of that seed. A change takes place in the mind and intellect of that sadhak. The body and the environment also respond according to the internal progress''.

In our system, the grace of the MOTHER that descends in the energy form, is the only help of the highest kind. The NAME is a game played by HER. By HER instructions, the place of meditation and food etc. also change. There should be an urge and the MOTHER responds. The aspirant becomes peaceful.

In the same letter, Gurudev adds: ''viewed in the light of MANTRA, 'Om' is the seed and RAM also. There is difference in the process. The sound of 'OM' affects on centres different from the sound of RAM'. 'RAM' is appropriate to our system. It is full of life force and bene-diction. 'RAM' perades in me through and through with the help of this NAME, my wire becomes vibrant instantly. This can be availed of easily and effectively.

God possesses numerous names. All have their effects. The name that is provided by the guru, traditionally at the time of initiation, possesses the active energy of that invested god, and the same appears in the Sadhak from seed to sappling and from blossoming to fruitation.

The RAM-MANTRA, that has been preached by Gurudev to us, has a long guru-tradition. The first initiator of this is Lord SHIVA.

The study of his works, his preachings and speeches have made us understand clearly that his system is based on SHAKTI PAT. The power, acquired through Mantra-Sadhana, leads the aspirant to the destination gradually according to the state of the sadhak. It takes the aspirant, by the holding his finger. The sadhak has only to submit himself fully the rest is done by the living power herself. The sadhak becomes amazed by looking at the wordeful lilas of that power, as an on looker.

When the energy is awakened by the grace of the guru, the Sadhak need not practise the ASANAS, PRANAYAN, MUDRA and nothing else. The KUNDALINI power when awakened tries its utmost to ascend to the Brahmarandhra, the seventh plexus. The small reactions that take place automatically, serve the purpose of the ASANAS and the PRANAYAM. When the Channel of power is energised, everything happens by itself. The Chitta becomes peaceful gradually. There have been some aspirants who never knew about the ASANAS and PRANAYAM, even in dreams, who had never gone through the YOG texts, had learnt no exercise, started doing these Kriyas as naturally as if they had practised them for years. It was possible only due to the awakened power. It astonisties one to see the Kriyas being performed by themselves. The more ashtonishing is the fact that only those Kriyas take place in the aspirant as are necessary for One. The Kriyas that require hard practise, do take place in the energised aspirant easily and effortlessly. The needed Pranayanes also happen and they succeed after some days in attempting then KUMBHAK easily. The Sadhak never feels harmed by these happenings. There is nothing like harmful because the awakened energy gets them done by itself as per the need of the Sadhak.

In the means of the Hathyogis, the path of Ascent, there are possibilities of danger to the sadhak through the smallest neglect or mistake. Therefore Hath Yog is forbidden unless there is some competent guide. But our system is that of DESCENT. The results of both are the same but this path is very safe and easy. There are only few fortunate who find guides to cause Shaktipat and help him in the realisation. If the SHAKTI is awakened once through the grace of guru, the self or God, the Shakti itself looks to the consumation of the aim of attainment. It may take any time but the awakened Shakti does not cease. The seed never decays. Of course, it may seem dormant sometimes due to unfavourable environment or due to the lack of means. The inner flow is always there.

The Shaktipat, having taken place, does not empower the Yogi to attempt any yogic-Kriya, with his own power, neither does his mind revel in that. He has to attempt only that which is inspired by the power. If he acts otherwise or disobeys his chitta shall not remain peaceful. As a man without sleep feels uneasy even on being healthy, so happens with such an aspirant. The aspirant feels happy and contented only on acting according to the instructions of the power. He has to go where it leads him to. The Shakti itself bears his burden. The Shakti always benefits him if his faith is full and firm.

SANT Gyaneshwar makes a very hearty and VIVID description of Shaktipat while annotating the two verses of the sixth chapter of Geeta. He writes:

"The one on whom this vision shines or whom the Lotus hand touches, even through he may be an ordinary being will shine like Maheshwar, Sanker. Lord Krishna had shown to ARJUN, His grand form by SHAKTIPAT only. When the Karma Vanishes, the guidecome to help by coming themselves. The Shakti pat done through sight or touch at the time of initiation by the Guru, leads the sadhak to the goal definitely.

The purpose of our sadhana is to awaken the soul and to make it appear face to face with God. The work of the Guru is to motivate the divine light in man and to work on. The mightly guru, glorifies the deserving disciple with his grace. An instance of Paramhans Ram Krishna and Vivekanand is worth hearing.

Once, while in the garden of Dakshineshwar, Guru dev made me sit peacefully and placed his hand on my head. Instantally I felt that the moon, the sun, the trees, the houses and the family have been dissolved in the space. Even the space appeared to have vanished. After that, what he saw is not fully remembered. But as I went on looking and looking, I was terror stricken. He could not withstand that and a shrick got out of my mouth. I asked in fear what it all was and where his parents were Gurudev said laughing that it was nothing and should stop. He patted my head with his hand again. I was amazed. The house, the family, the sun, the moon and the trees were there as usual. This kind of another experence he had in America.

Likewise our kind guru Ramanand also rained his bliss on his sadhaks in the camp at SIHI in 1949 and 50 to the great amazement and contentment of the sadhakas. He had showered such favours on his followers at other places also and even in his astral body now, he is obliging many off and on. These who were fortunate enough to he near the guru at the time of his last retreat and who had real faith and deserving, were blessed by the gurudeva with his full powers.

Swami Vivekanand describes another such instance at the time of the passing away of Ram Krishna Parama Hansa :

"The gurudeva, called me to him alone, before two or three days before his departure. He made me still before him and tooked at me altentively. He went into Samadhi then and there. I, immediately felt that a subtle ball of light with the sharp shine of the lightning emanated from the body of gurudeva and entered my body. After some time, I also lost the external knowledge and recognition. I could not know how long it took to be so. When my worldly consciouness returned, I saw that gurudeva was crying. He said affectionally that he had given away to me, everything what he had. He shall be redeemed of this obligation only when he will benefit the world with this power. I think that very power of the guru, makes me do all that I do. This body is not now to sit and rest.''

When the incarnations, come down to this world they come with a purpose of the liberated souls, to help in their Lilas. They attain personal forms and bodies for the good of all.

Our guru also was an incarnated soul. Numerous sadhak rallied round him to partake his Lilas. No place in India has been left whereform sadhaks did not come to him? All have been blessed by him. Every one feels that he is a favourite of guru. He was like a sun and the reflections of his grace feel on that mirror of heart which was the clearest.

The system that has down to us through our guru is wonderful in itself but it is reasonable and timely. Of the Shaktipat of the amazing interactions due to the rise of the Kundalani power, the mention of which had been made by me above, has been a matter of realisation by the saints and the sages since the vedic period such references are commonly found in the vedas, shastras, upanishads and in the works of Shankaracharya. Ramakrishna Param Hans, Vijai Krishna Goswami, his disciple Kuldanand, and many other modern sages acquired Kundalini shakti through Shaktipat and with that divine power helped in the bringing out of a new era. Some saints are of the opinion that without the upsurage of the Shakti, entrance to the path of Sadhna is impossible. Those who do not Know fully about this call this system anti-shastra. But the Ramayan clearly says :

''Without knowing, there cannot be belief. Unless there is belief, there cannot be any Lone. Without Lone there is no devotion. It is like the paste of water.''

The one who has received the path with the blessings of the guru, whose mysterious powers have awakened, doubtfree. The realisation of the spiritual element praised openly in the upanishads, makes one feel fulfilled.

The Sadhak ascending this path step by step, One day realises the Adwait Tatwa with the grace of the Great Power. The realised ones say that the dorment power opens its eyes and the sadhaks enters into the world of Super consciousness. All the system of the day are invariably the various efforts to open this grate of Godhood.

The worship of the Param is the real worship. The unity or merger into Param Shiva is the worship Divine.

Our System of Worship

What is worship?

Worship (Upasana) is the sadhana that is performed for being one with the great mother, for developing devotion in the feet of God and for self evolution, by sitting each day for one or two hours.

Cleanliness

Though there is no hard and fast rule yet it is better to sit for worship after cleaning and washing hands and mouth and feet as it helps in concentration. If bath is taken, it is still better.

Time

The Naam Jap may be continued any time but a time has to be fixed for sitting for worship. One feels hungry at the time when one takes his food daily. Similarly the urge of worship also arises at the usual time. So it is better to sit for worship and meditation at some appainted time. The ideal time for worship is said to be two and half hours before sun rise which is thought to be 'Brahm Muhurt'. If its not possible, efforts should be made to get up as early as possible before sun rise. One may sit for worship in the evening also at the time of sun set. Those who have no such facility, may avoid it. The final decision should be taken by the sadhak himself according to his circumstances, facilities, physical conditions and cease. The time once fixed should not be changed or ignored.

Place

It would be better if the place of worship is a saparate room which is not used for any other purpose. A place far from any sound or interference is preferable.

Seat (Aasan)

The seat should be so as to enable the descent of the great power and to facilitate the exercises for the ascent of power. All decisions will have to be taken keeping these things in view. Sitting cross leged is an easy posture. Those who are used to may sit in Sidhasan or Padmasan. It is said "Sthir Sukhamasanam," meaning thereby that the Aasan should be comfortable. At the time of sitting the body should be kept in balance. A change may take place in the asan automatically, when interactions of power take place. Efforts should not be made to stop them. Its possible that the body may turn, the neck may bend, the body may tilt towards any side. The spinal cord may be sometimes straight and sometimes bent. If the aasan is uncomfortable, uneaisness may be felt at the time of interactions. Under such condition the posture may be changed according to the inspiration. It is proper that the fingers intertwined may be placed in the lap. Those who feel comfortable may place their hands on their knees. The body should be effortless and there should be an urge from insight. Only these two are the last rules. The ability to sit in one pasture for long develops gradually.

Declaration

Before sitting into meditation a resolve should be made for the period for which the sitting is to continue. The rest may be decided later on.

Dharna

For the sitting, in the begining stage, Dharna is very necessary. The rememberance for God or the thought of his omnipotence creates a proper condition of mind for the mantra. Any prayer or sincere prostration may do this work.

It is necessary that the presence of God or his great power should be felt very close. It is better if it is thought that the power is descending on. It will be still better if it is thought that he is sitting in the lap of the great mother. At the time of sitting, the mother should be invoked by bowing his head and saying. "Mother, lead me to where you like, in the way you like as you take to the external world, take me similarlly to the inner one. You know better my interests. Let your wish be fulfilled."

It should be thought that God is before him is on the right and on the left, on the back and all arround. The Sadhak should feel himself in the lap of the mother. We may just concentrate on the Nirakar Swaroop or Jyoti Swaroop of God. The Ram Naam in the Word form may also be made the object of the concentration.

Lighting

A light should be kindled reverently and after sitting. The name of Ram should be pronounced three times loudly. Its viberation will render the atmosphere favourable to meditation.

Prayer

After that, a prayer should be made arousing the sense that the mother may cause Divinity to reign or that the meditator is a child and the power his mother. Invocation and a call should start next.

Invocation (Awahan)

The invocation should be done slowly, faithfully and understanding the sense fully. In a group jap, only the leader should chant the mantra. In individual cases the invocation should be extended individually in the following words:-

''O, Sri Ram, the lord of lords, you are pure, enlightened, eternal, omnipatent, the embodiment of Sacchidananda and the only one God. Param Purush, the kindest and the greatest, I bow to thee again and again.''

At the time of inviting the feeling should continue that the call is being made respectfully to the Istdev by remembering his grand attributes. It should be felt that those attributes are developing in him. If the Istdev apears in the vision, it should be offered compliments reverently.

Namashkar Saptak

The following Namaskar should be recited loudly together by all the worshipers

करते हैं हम बन्दना, नत शिर बारम्बार।
तुझे देव! परमात्मन! मंगल शिव शुभकार।।
अँजलि पर मस्तक किये, विनय भक्ति के साथ।
नमस्कार मेरा तुझे, होवे जग के नाथ।।
दोनों कर को जोड़कर, मस्तक घुटने टेक।
तुझको हो प्रणाम मम, शत शत कोटि अनेक।।
पाप हरण, मंगल करण, चरण शरण का ध्यान।
धार करूँ प्रणाम मैं, तुझको शक्ति निधान।।
भक्ति भाव शुभ भावना, मन में भर भरपूर।
श्रद्धा से तुझको नमूं, मेरे राम हजूर।।
ज्योतिर्मय जगदीश हे! तेजोमय अपार।

परमपुरुष पावन परम, तुझको हो नमस्कार।।
सत्यज्ञान आनन्द मय, परम धाम श्री राम।
पुलकित हो मेरा तुझे, होवे बहु प्रणाम।।"

After the prayer is over, the group leader may recite the Ram Naam for three times loudly. This should be followed by the Nam Jap silently for about forty minutes, or so depending upon the conditions and circumstances.

The individual meditators continue their Jap, concentrating at the light form of God. Some try to concentrate on the waves produced by the word 'Ram'. Some associate the word Ram with the coming and goning of the breath. Some concentrate at the written form of the word Ram'

'Amrit Vani' explanes about the Jap with the help of breath:

"राम नाम घट भीतर बसे
साँस–साँस नस–नस से रसे,
सपने में भी न बिसरे राम
राम–राम श्री राम–राम–राम।"

Tulsidaas has also described a special method of the Jaap of Ram Mantra–

"तुलसी 'र' के कहत ही, निकसत पाप पहाड़
फिर भीतर आवत नहीं, देत मकार किवाड़।"

When the breath goes in then 'रा' and when it goes out, (म) should be pronounced silently. With this practice, the pranayam takes place and it shows a wonderful result.

The close of Upasana:–

When the period of the sitting is over, the leader should pronounce. Ram Naam to bring a close to the upasana. The leader may sing prayers according to his wish. The following blessings brings a close of the sitting:

"सर्वे भवन्तु सुखिनः, सर्वे सन्तु निरामयाः,
सर्वे भद्राणि पश्यन्तु, मा कश्चिद दुःख भाग्भवेत्।।"

All should he happy; All should be free from mental afflictions: All should see the good and none should be miserable.

"न तोऽहम् कामयेराज्यम्, न स्वर्गम न पुनर्भवम्,
कामऐ दुःखतप्तानाम्, प्राणि नामार्ति नाशनम्।।"

I wish not a kingdom: I aspire not for heaven or Moksha. My only wish is that I should be able to redeem the sufferer from grief.

"त्वदिष्टम् भवतु गोविन्द!
"त्वदिष्टम् भवतु गोविन्द!
"त्वदिष्टम् भवतु गोविन्द!

Govind! Let your wish be fullfilled

ॐ शान्ति, शान्ति, शान्ति।

The Most Powerful Mother

The controlling power of the world and space is called MAHAMAYA, MAHASHKTI OR KUNDALIN SHAKTI and a light ray of that power. Lives in the human body at a particular place and controlls it. This power is called Kundalini.

The realised yogis and the sadhaks have a practical experience of the fact that it is full of endless power. Those sadhaks who are successful in awakening this power, find before them a great store of divine power.

Whatever there is in the store of cosmos, is also present in the human body in a subtler form. The sun, the moon, the planets, and the stars, the spheres and the divinities, the sidhas and the mahatmas, are all in it. As the Chandliers and the bulbs embllish with the touch of the electronic switch, similarly the inner part of the sadhak becomes illuminated and is filled with power at the time of awakening of the Kundalini. He gets entry into new divine spheres. He enjoys himself the divine bliss by withnessing celestial scenes, by hearing celeslial sounds, and by testing divine rasas, by smelling divine odours and by feeling divine touches. An ordinary person, can not even think of it. When he hears such experiences from others, he simply gets bewildered, and exclaims :

कहहुं न कर कछु युक्ति विशेषी।
यह सब मैं, निज नयनन देखी।।

''All that has been seen by my own eyes, is beyond description.''

As भू (Bhu) (Bhuwah), Swah, Mahak, Janah, Tapah, and Satyan spheres lie in the outer space, in the some way, in the body space also, exist seven spheres which are described as seven chakras or plexus. They are six i.e. Muladhar, Swadhisthan, Manipur, Anahat, Vishudha, Agya placed in the different parts of the body whereas the seventh Sahasrar, is situated at the top of the head.

These Chakras are closely related with the seven external spheres. Now, our consciousness is centred at the Muladhar. Therefore our contact goes on with the Bhulok i.e. world sphere. But when the Kundalini is aroused and it moves upwards through Sushumna, the upper chakras start opening. The first stroke at the Muladhar, presses upon the genitals. Therefore Moolbandh is very necessary at this time. After the opening of the Muladhar Chakra, the Sadhak enters the Subtile world from physical body, starts moving towards sushumna. All the spheres are squeezed inside. At that time Bhasrika Pranayam starts taking place, the thighs seem to stretch upwards. The sadhak should sustain himself boldly at this time. He should never feel terrified.

At the time of the ascending of the Kundalini, there appears wonderful lights of Nadis, Chakras, tanmatras, and other elements like those of the electricity and the sadhak becomes suprised. The sounds of the Subtle world also become audible, which are termed as 'Anahad Nad'. A never heard music is also listened to. In the beginning it is like the sound of the Crickets. It is followed by the sounds of a bell, a gong, Jhanjh, Miradarg flute, and conch etc. The musical instruments that are played upon into our temples, at the time of Arati, are all represented through these sounds. These instruments indicate the opening of the gates of the Temple and the darshan of the deity. Similarly these subtle sounds indicate the experience of having the vision of God, living inside the human heart. A mysterious change starts taking place in the Sadhak. He should watch these sounds reverently. Kabir deseribes his experiences happily in the following words :–

"शून्य महल में दिया बारले, आसन सों मत डोल रे।
कहै कबीर, आनंद भयों है, बाजत अनहद ढोल रे।।

Absorbed in these sounds day and night, he sings out his experiences:

शब्द निरंतर सौं मन लाग्या, मलिन वासना त्यागी।
ऊठत, बैठत, कबहुंन छूटत, ऐसी ताली लागी।।

In the saint-philosophy, Anahad Sound occupies a great importance. It is akin to the sound of the flute of Krishna.

बाजत अनहद बासुंरी, तिरवेनी के तीर।
राग छतीसो हो रहे, गरजत गगन गंभीर।।

Another saint asserts:

अनहद शब्द भंवर गुंजारैं, संख परवावज बाजैं।
ताल घंट, मुरली घन घोरा, भेरि दमामे गाजैं।।

सिद्ध गर्जना अतिहो भारी, घुंघरू गति झनकारैं।
रंभान्नत्य करैं विन पगसूं, विन पायल ठनकारैं।
गुरू सुखदेव करैं जब किरिया, ऐसा नाम दिखावैं।
चरनदास वा पग के परसैं, आवागमन नसावैं।

This anahad sound dialating every where should be merged with the sound of the Ishta mantra and the Sadhak should become absorbed in listening to the same.This sound creates miracles lateron. In 'The Amritbani', it is started:

कुंडलनी बोधे, सुषम्ना खोले।
राम नाम अमृत रस घोले।।
उपजे नाद सहज बहु भांती।
अजपा जाप, भितर हो शांती।।

''When Kundalini awakes, Sushana opens. It pours out nectlar of Ram Nam. Differcut kinds of sounds come out. Inner peace comes by Ajapa Jap.''

It means that the Jap becomes automatic by uniting with the sound of Anahad, Ram or the Oum mantra, resulting in permanant peace.

This sound comes from different spheres and brings with it the spatial attributes to adore the sadhaks with them.

The sadhak is blessed with this divine bliss. The subtle world is stranger than the physical world. The subtlity and wonderfulness of that sphere may terrify the sadhak in the beginning. But there is no need to be afraid of. It is a pass to the divine bliss.

Once the Kundalini is awakened it should not be thought that the same shall ever happen. The fitness of mind and body, purity, sutlity and the sanctity of thoughts is very necessary. In the absence of these, the process will cease.

If the Kundalini stays itself into one of the Chakras it should not be thought that it has been awankened fully. The awakening of the kundalini shall be complete only when the pranic flow of the astral body enters the Sushuma and the material body and would also enter the astral field by becoming so. During this stage Brahmacharya, self control, pure diet and living and thinking are imperative otherwise this invaluable treasure shall disappear.

Effulgent lights do appear at this state. The astral body goes to different spheres and experiences divine scenes, meets divine beings,

Sidhas, gods and feel, divine Odours and tastes. They should be looked upon gratefully but disinterestedly like Drashta (witness) only. It is never desirable to be absorbed in them.

These mysterious experiences should be kept a secret An ordinary person can not understand them. So they become blind believers and are duped by the false ones. The sadhak develops ego and the desire of praise also.

Now, the question arises how to have this immense treasure?

There are two ways. The one is called AROH PATH, the other, 'AVAROH'. In the Aroh path, the sadhak endeavows himself by learning the process through the Guru, some saint or satsang. The Ashtang Yog system comes under it. In it Yama, Niyam i.e. non-Violence, Truth, Astya (non-stealing), Brahma-Charya Aparigrah (Non-hoarding) are yamas. They bring inner purity. Shaunch (cleanliness) Santosh, Top, Swadhyaya and submission to God, are Niyam. They bring external purity. These are the stepping stones of the Yog-structured.

After this, for the strength and the development of physical body, different kinds of Aasnas and for the increase of inner strength, control of pranic powers or pranayam should be resorted to. Then Pratyahar is the effort of concentrating the senses on one point, followed by Dharana, i.e. fixing some point for meditation should be practised. The Dhyeya or the point of concentration, may be a light a picture and idol or mantra or thought according to the desire of the sadhak.

Then contemplation (Dhyan) begins. In this process, the object of dharna has to be fixed upon by the mind. The matured condition of contemplation leads to Samadhi. The samadhi is of two types, Savikalpa and Nirvikalpa. In the savikalpa, state of samadhi, a distinction exists between the sadhak and the sadhya. The sadhak does not completely identify himself with the Dhyey. But in the Nirvikalpa state of samadhi, all the three, Dhyata (Meditator), Dhyan, (Contemplation) and Dhyeya, (the object) become one. It seems that the drop, has become an ocean itself by merging into the ocean. In this system the internal and external Sanyam and the observance of the yogic rules, is very necessary. This path is subject to fulfilment by ones own efforts. Here the ascent takes place from down to upwards. Therefore, this is termed Aroh path. The other path is that of submission. In this path reverence and faith are needed for the grace of the Ishia (deity); of the Guru and for the mantra. When the mantra initiated by the Guru is repeated faithfully, the divine consciousness guides the path of the sadhak by itself. He has to make a complete surrender before it. This path requires devotion for the Guru fait in the mantra and the total submission. It is said:

देव कृपा स्वशक्ति का सहस्त्र कमल में मिलाप।
हो सत्पुरुष संयोग से, सकल नष्ट हों पाप।।

"The self power unites with the SAHASRAR-kamal by the grace of God. When such a communion takes place all the sin decay dwindle.

It is a very wonderful thing that the kundalini awakens by itself when the power of the mantra given by the Guru begins to react. The power of the mantra makes, the sadhak observe the Astrtang yog system of its own. It all happens and is not done. The sadhak no longer remains the doer. He becomes the observer and the mantra becomes alive and the kundalini is awakened. It is very difficult to find such Gurus, but it should be remembered that as the seeker endeavours to find the Guru, similarlly, the guru also remains in search of the proper disciple. Both of them, attract each other. If the follower has an intense desire and faith, he will get a guru easily and the power of the Guru will start transforming him.

Let us now discuss the form and the situation of kundalini. Out of a large number of Naadis, the Sushumna is the best. It runs through the Spinal Cord like an invisible canal. Inside the Sushumna, there is a Nadi, called Bajra, then there is Chitrani and in the last, the Brahm Nadi. All these Nadies are very fine like the thread of the Spider. The Yogies only know them. Even a Microscope can not see them. These Nadies are full of Satva elements, are full of light and full of power. There are several centres of these Nadis. Where many Nadies conjunct, the centre is called the Padma (Lotus) or Kamal Chakra. Out of these centres, the fallowing seven are the main ones. (1) Muladhar. (2) Swadhishthan, (3) Manipurak. (4) Anahat (5) Vishudha (6) Agya and (7) Sahasrar. These Chakras (Plexus) are the stores of power. In their ordinary state, these chakras remain drooping down and in an unbloomed condition. They give vent to their powers when they are aroused with the help of Jap, Dhyan and other spiritual practices. Description of these chakras, has been made in detail in the books on Hathyog. Raj Yog or Tantra Yog. But there is no need of knowing their details. The following ordinary knowledge of them is sufficient.

1. MULADHAR :

This chakra is situated about an inch above the anus and about one inch below the genital. It has four petals, is red in colour and has four letters, वं, शं, षं, सं, (Vam, Sham, Kham, and Sam). These letters shine like melted gold. Its element is earth and the deity is Indra or the vahan is Airavat (The elephant) of Indra. Those sadhaks who awaken their kundalini by the devotion of chakras, they worship them properly. They appear before the sadhak in the state of meditation. The Sadhak is bewilders to witness these mysterious things which appear by the grace of the Guru and by the Jap of the Mantra. I have my personal associations with some of such sadhaks who have actually experienced these myracles.

Like the Muladhar the other chakras also have different number of petals, colours, power-letters, deities, vehicles and elements. The total number of such petals is fifty. All the vowels and the consonants of Hindi, fifty numbers are inscribed on these chakras. On the Vishudha chakra which is placed in the throat, has sixteen petals of all the Hindi Vowels from अ to अः. The Anahat Chakra has twelve petals consisting of twelve consonants from क to ठ. The ten petals of Manipurak have ten letters from ड to फ, The six petals of the swadhishthan possess consonants from ढ़ to ल; the four petals of Muladhar have four letters from ब to स and the two petals of the Agya Chakra have the two letters ह and क्ष inscribed on it. All these letters are full of nasal sounds (अनुस्वार), i.e. कं, बं etc.

From Muladhar to Vishudha Chakra there is the spchere of the five elements, earth water, fire, Air, and Sky. These are the five elements of the chakras in Seriatim. The Agya chakra is the sphere of the mend and the intellect. The deities related to these elements have their vehicles accordingly. Some Sadhaks arouse the chakras by worshipping them properly. But in our system of worship, the mantra 'Ram given by the Guru and its sound and the dhyan of Ram, awaken the chakras automatically and bless the sadhak with the same results as he gets by hard yogic penance.

When the Muladhar Chakra is energised, the sadhak developes in him a feeling of inner joy and the power of composing sentences, verses and great epics. It has been described in the Yog and the tantra books that the Brahma Nadi, inside the Sushumna has the Swayam bhuling a near it; where the kundalini lies dorment like the folds of a Conch in three and a half rounds. The Mulshakti or the basis of the power of the Kundalini, earns the name of Muladhar for this reason. This great kundalini power resides in the body of every being. The whole cosmos is lit with the light of this kundalini. By the grace of guru, the kundalini awakens slowly and slowly, enabling the sadhak to proceed on the spiritual both hurriedly. This chakra is related to the earth.

2. SWADHISTHAN

This Chakra is placed Two anguls (inches) near the Abdomen this is the second Chakra, Swadhisthan having six petals. It has six letters on them. It is concerned with the Bhuvah (भुव) sphere. It means that when Swathisthan is energised, it associates the sadhak with the Bhuvah sphere. When this plexus or chakra is aroused, the Godess Saraswati descends on the tongue of the Sadhak invariably.

3. MANIPUR

The third Chakra is Manipur. It's place of location is the root of the nave. It's Lotus has ten petals. It's energising produces internal knowledge. Concentration (Dhyan) on this chakra, cures ailments like the loss of appetite etc. It increases vitalily. This chakra is very important for meditation purposes. The great mantra of the Budha 'ॐ मणिपद्मे हुय' is associated with it. This is the store house of manis (Precious Stones) of the spiritual world. The Brahma Granthi is placed there when this Chakra is energised the sadhak feels the flames of fire as the cool cushions. This is related to the heavenly sphere स्व (Swah)

4. ANAHAT CHAKRA

This Chakra is placed near the heart and is like the lotus with twelve petals. When it is energised great powers like versification, self discipline, hearing celestial sounds and increase of devotional thoughts, take place. This Chakra is very important for SAGUN UPASAKS. This Chakra is the spot of SHABDA BRAHMA, ONKAR VISHNU GRANTHI is located here. It is related with MAHARLOK.

5. VISHUDHA CHAKRA

It's Spot is the throat. It's force is like the Sixteen petalled lotus. It's awakening makes one a poet, a sage, and a peaceful, healthy grieftess and long living man. This Chakra is the spot of MANAS and therefore the mind become space like, for this reason it is called VISHUDHA. It's petals bear sixteen vowels from 'अ' to अः. It is the gate of heaven for the worshipper. It relates to JANALOK.

6. AGYA CHAKRA

It is placed at the joint of the two eye brows, inside the BHRAKUTI. It is like the lotus, with two petals. The result, of the other Chakras, are obtained by concentrating only on this chakra. It gives the ability to attain ASAMPRAGYAT SAMANY.

The NADIS, IDA, PINGALA and SHUSHUMNA emanate separately from the MULADHAR and they make a confluence at this place. So, this spot is called YUKTA TRIVENI (Sangam of the three). IDA is Ganga, PINGLA, Yamuna and sushumna is SARASWATI. This is Sangam, Tirthraj or Triveni where one gets riddance from all sins after bathing in them. It is said:

इडा, भगीरथी गंगा पिंगला यमुना नदी।
तयोर्मध्यगता नाडी, सुसुम्णा, सरस्वती ।।
त्रिवेणी संगमो यम, तीर्थराज स उच्चयते ।
तम स्नानं कृत्वा, सर्व पाप्मैः प्रमुच्यते ।।

This AGYA CHAKRA is like the Third eye of Lord SHIVA. It's opening destroys the desire completly. KAM is burnt down:

तब शिव तीसर नैन उधारा ।
चितवत काम भयउ जरि छारा ।।

KAM, Lives but it trans forms into purity. The deity of this Chakra, is Lord Shiva. The sanyam on this Chakra, Creates in the sadhak a strong will power. The RUDRA GRANTHI is supposed to the located here. If this granthi is not dissolved, the body weakens but the TEJ increases. The Kundalini power associates with Param Shiva, at the SAHASRAR. It is related to TAPAHLOK.

7. SAHASRAR

There is a centre of all the nerves in the brain, above the palate. It is like a lotus with thousand petals. At this spot, when pran and intellect conjunct all the Vrittis come to a standstill and the sadhak gains the ability of attaining SAMPRAGYAT Samadhi. The upanishads describe the self (Hridpurush) equal to one angula (अगुल), existing in this place. The Sadhak enjoys himself of the bliss when all the vrittis subside at the calming down of the PRAN and the mind. The experience of being one with God, is gained here. Kabir writes:

जल में कुंभ, कुंभ में जल है, बाहर भीतर पानी।
फूटा कुंभ, जल जलहि समाना, यह तत कहऊ ज्ञानी।।

"The pitcher is into the water, and the water is into the pitcher. All around there is water and water alone. When this pticher is broken, water Units with water. This reality is known by the wise only."

The purpose of the human body is solely to achieve this state. The aspirants who attain this state through the Yogic powers, reach the State of PARAMHANSAS, i.e., liberated ones.

This SAHASRAR is called the sphere of SATYA, (Truth). An idiot became wise, and full of Pragya (reality) after attaning this state. The shastras (books of wisdom) became handballs of such sadhaks. The gates of knowledge open apart and the stream of knowledge flows from his mouth. The great scholars are surprised at his deliberations.

All this is the result of establishing the KUNDALINI, into SAHASRAR, after its energisation. The, SHUSHUNA, lies aspleep in the Ordinary state with its power. Only the flow of Pranic energy continues through Ida and Pingala nadis. But by spiritual sadhana, the grace of the guru, The Mantra Jap, internal and external purity, the kundalini enters the Sushumna and ascends upwards to SAHASRAR the channel of divine consciousness opens. This power has been described like a serpent having two months. One month is kept closed (to lie steeping) with its tail. The breathing is done with the other. The action of of Kundalini is not visible externally. In reality the existence of kundalini is like a girdled serpent, like an unseen NADI. It has been said in the Shastras:

"मूलाधारे सर्पवत् कुंडलीकृता नाड़ी वर्त्तमाने तत्मध्ये
स्थापित्वात् इयं कुंडलिनी" (शारदातिलक टीका)

The Awakening of Kundalini

The meaning of the awakening of the Kundalini is the flowing of PRAN SHAKTI into Shushumna upwards under the influence of the Mantra power. As, the electical appliances and wires fitted in a room, start working at the switching the plug on similarly, the Kundalini switch energises the wire of sushumna. The chakra, where kundalini connection reaches blooms fully rising upwards. When the Kundalini reaches, Agya Chakra, the State of SAMPRAGYAT SAMADHI Occurs and when it reaches the SAHASRAR, ASAMPRAGYAT Samadhi is attained. Under this State, a man becomes full of incredible knowledge and experences. Those divine things should not be described to everyone.

THE METHOD

Specially, The kundalini awakens through pure body, pure thoughts, pure heart pure love for God, total renunciation, deep meditation or contemplation. If miracles in extra ordinary are noticed this state should be thought to be the result of the Sanskars of the previous birth. This state is also experienced when some mysterous happening awakens the kundalini. The satsang of the great persons, other blessings, the grace of the guru, the power of the mantra, the divinity and formal Yogic efforts performed faithfully also help in the attainment of Mahashakti to help the awakening of the Kundalini.

Our path is the path of surrender where there is little need of self efforts. The Jap of Ram Nam, the blessings of the guru and the grace of God are necessary for the descent of super consciousness. This super-consciousness (महाशक्ति) inspires the soul power to unite with the SAHASRAR completely.

'Amrit Vani,' States rightly:

देव दया, स्वशक्तिका सहस्त्रकमल में मिलाप।
हो सत्पुरुष संयोग से, सकल नष्ट हो पाप।।

"The self-power (स्वशक्ति) units with the SAHASRAR Kamal by the grace of God and this communion leads to the decay of all sins."

The Secret of Self-Realisation

(The State of Consciousness, TURIYAWASTHA)

There are four states of our consciousness (or life), JAGRAT (State of awakening), Swapna (the State of sleep), Sushupti, (the State of deep sleep) and TURIYA, (the State of egolessness). In Islamic musticism hey are called NASUT (नासूत), MALKUT (मलकूत), JABRUT (जबरूत) and LAHUT (लाहूत). In the State of Turiya, the consciousness turns inside. A further progress in this state comes the feeling of 'AHAM BRAHMASMI (I am God) appears. Islam calls it ANALHAQ (अमहलक). The aim of SUFI sadhana is to possess this state. They have expressed in their works:

पहुंचा जो आपको तो मैं पहुंचा खुदा के तई।
मालूम अब हुआ कि मैं बहुत दूर था ।।

"The farness from God, is realised by the sadhak only when he reaches God."

In that State, everything seems pervaded by God. He feels that all this universe is a manifestation of God only ("सर्वं खलु इदं ब्रह्म".) Iqbal, the famous Urdu poet, explains in his Marfat Verses:

बाये नादानी। कि तू मोहताजे साकी हो गया।
मय भी तू, मीना भी तू, साकी भी तू, महफिल भी तू।।

"It is a thing of great ignorance that the wine is asked for from the server. Realise your own self. The reality is that he himself is wine, the cup and the cup-bearer as well."

Another Verse says:

कांपता है दिल तेरा, अंदेशये तूफां से क्यों?
ना खुदा तू, बहर तू, किश्ती भी तू, साहिल भी तू।।

Standing on the shores why are you afraid with the coming of the shore. why are your afraid with the coming of the shores. Realise yourself, you are the ocean, the boat and the sailor yourself, even as the shores is. When you are all where the fear is!

आह! किसकी जुश्तजू, आवारा रखती है तुझे।
राह तू, रहबर भी तू, रहदा भी तू, मंजिल भी तू।।

O, Where are you wandering seeking whom? Remove your curtain of confusion and look you are the path, the traveller, the guide and the goal. In the fourth state of Turiya the gates of divine knowledge open apart. Divine consciousness become alive and the state of sahaj Samadhi is reached. The sadhak then realises that the would of name and form, which he had thought to be real so far is only an illusion. The truth is Brahma itself. The picture is not real, the artist only is real.

जो नक्स है हस्तीका, धोखा नजर आता है।
परदे पे मुसव्विर हो, तनहा नजर आता है।।

"The existence painted on the canvas is illusion, the painter only is reality."

The same thing has been said by our Shastrakara's also.

"B ब्रह्मसत्यं, जगन्मिथ्या" The reality is God only; the world is illusion. The real form is He everyother thing is only reflection. The form is visible through the reflections. A person feeling like this sees God in everything and every being. Shri Shanker Acharya says:

मुझमें तुझमें, और अन्य में, व्याप्त एक ही विष्णु।
अतः वृथा तू क्रोधित होता है, मुझ पर असहिष्णु।।
आत्मरूप परमेश्वर को ही, सब जीवों में जान।
अबसे भी सर्वत्र त्याग दे, भेदभाव का ज्ञान।।

"The same God (विष्णु), lives in you and I. Therefore it is useless to be intolerent and angry. Treat God living in all beings and give up the feeling of differences.

An Urdu, poet asserts nicely:

शक्ले इंसा में खुदा था, मुझे मालूम न था।
चांद बादल में छिपा था, मुझे मालूम न था।।

अगर्रचे इन्सान खुदा नहीं।
मगर खुदा इन्सान से जुदा नहीं।।

"One does not know that God is in the figure of man, like the moon, cancealed in the clouds." ''Although man is not God; but God is not separate from man.''

As long as the sadhak had no vision of God and his consciousness was extrovert he was under illusion. But when the curtain of ignorance is removed, he feels convinced that the world is only a tale that can not be told usefully.

"दुनिया से एक अफसाना कहने कोथे, फिर सोचा।
दुनिया है खुद अफसाना, अफसाने को क्या कहिए।।

When the inner vision of the person opens, he begins to understand the reality of the world and its relationship with God. Then, he begins to feel the futility of the wordly objects. Even the grandears of the grandiers become nothing to him.

"खुल गया जिसये राज़े पिन्हानी।
हेच उसकी है, ऐश सुल्तानी।"

"The kingly riches are ash, in comparision to the secret of Bliss to the persan who has come to know the reality"

Swami Ram Tirtha says:

बादशाह दुनियां के हैं, मोहरे तेरी शतरंज के।
दिल्लगी से चाल है, सामने सुलहो जंग के ।।

"The kings of the world, are the 'Muharas' of the chess. All the movements are fake."

The person who has eageness for God realisation, is always absorbed in his quest of God. He delves deep into the search of who am I? and forgets everything of the external world. He feels himself before the eternal, unending omnipresent power, forgetting everything.

The self realisation or the visions of God, do not occur at the surfacial level of our consciousness. They take place in the fourth State of TURIYA or in the Samadhi Chetna. The sadhana is celebrated to achieve that state. Meditation on self is done peacefully after getting up early in the morning.

Let ûs ponder deeply on this point.

When we sit for meditation or Jap, in a temple or elsewhere, the flow of thoughts born of sanskaras, starts. This flow is of the Chitta Vrittis that continues unabated. If this flow stops the entery into Yog-Marg will start. Therefore the Yog-Sutrakar says: योगः चित्रवृत्ति निरोधः। The next aphornism is "तदा दृष्टुः स्वरूपे अववस्थानम', Which means that the sadhak establishes himself into his 'self' form. He begins to know his reality. The problem of, who am I?" dissolves. He begins to feel that he is the controller of his vrittis when the vrittis are pacified, and the reality is understood, the mis-understanding that 'I am body', also goes away. So long as this feeling of bodiness is existant, the realisation is not complete when the 'Nirodh' State becomes Akhand, the realisation of self-establishment also becomes firm. The feeling of bodiness goes away for ever.

Those who have attained 'Swarupawastha' do not have any 'Dehadhyas', i.e., the feeling of Bodily pride. His Satwick activities go on peacefully. The awareness, the carefulness and the disinterestedness of self realisation appears in every action and behaviour of the sadhak. Kabir has defined this state as SAHAJ SAMADHI.

साधौ, सहज समाधि भली।
गुरु प्रताप जा दिन से जागी, दिन दिन अधिक चली।
सुखदुख से कोई परे, परमपद् तेह पद रहा समाई।।

"SAHAJ Ṣamadhi is the best. When this samadhi state is attained with the grace of Guru, it becomes firm and firm further. This state is beyod happiness and unhappiness.

Tulsidas explains:

रघुपति भगति करत कठिनाई।
कहत सुगम करनी अपार जानिहि सोई जाहि बनि आई।।

"The devotion of Ram, is very difficult. It is very easy to say but hard in performance. Only those come to realisation who are fortunate enough."

The yogi, established in Brahma Bhawa remains in samadhi Chetna or Turiyavastha. The visible world is dissolved into him. He lives in the state of Adwait and enjoys himself the bliss of Brahmabhav (ब्रह्मभाव). This State is without any grief, greed fear, happiness, day and night place and time. Brahma is felt everywhere. Tulsidas says that unless this state is achieved the delusions do not subside. This state is possible with Yukti (युक्ति) and not shakti (शक्ति).

According to the, "Patanjali Yog Darshan" Turiyavastha, or Samadhi State needs total submission to God, the best way.

समाधि सिद्धि ईश्वर प्राणिधानात्।

The Sadhana of Ramanandji is fully based on surrender to God. He has discussed the Samadhi Chetna or Turiya Vastha, in detail in his book "ADHIYATMAK SADHANA," He asserts.

"The consciouness lying beyond inellect is called Samadhi Chetna. It is full of realisations. But they appear in a strange way. In the wake of this knowledge power, all the mysteries of the world become known. The 'self' hidden behind all the elements becomes visible.

There is another aspect of knowledge beyond, ie. the union with God. The Sadhak who reaches this state, feels the presence of God, in everything and in every being. Swami Satyanand says", The visit of NACHIKETA to YAMA and receiving instructions from him is an event having taken place in Turiya Vastha. That is a state of internal sphere, beyond the senses. Only Divyabhawas works there. The difference between this state and the dream state is that every thing is true in this state as against everything false in the dream state. In this other worldly state, there is Divya Samadhi fully. The feeling of time and place is felt fully. In that State, NACHIKETA, feel is going to YAMA, seeing him and being instructed by him. This state was achieved by Nachiketa, suddenly by the wordpower of Bajsvava. He got it just as his father said that he head given him to Yamaraj. He witnessed all the scenes in his astrol form of body. After meeting and talking to yama, he returned to his physical form which lay in his father's house in the meantime. The father only thought that he had wokup from sleep.

The divine pranks seen by Kag Bhushundi (कागभुशुण्डि) after entering the mouth of Ram, were the result of this samadhi chetna. Markandeya also saw the scene of PRALAYA (The great deluge), under this state, with the grace of God. Shri Krishna made Arjun see his grand form in this very state.

When this turiyavastha is reached wih the grace of the guru, self, God etc. the sadhak becomes Capable of witnessing divine visions, divine sounds, visiting astral spheres in his sukshma body, and meeting sidhas and other gods. It is a very wonderful state. The experiences of this state are also wonderful. The Characterstics of Turiyavastha, have been described by Ram Kinkar is in his book "The Beauty of Sundarkand', in the following words.

"Any second desire in life does not arise, unless the first one is satisfied i.e. the next vrathi, arises only after the first one subsides.

This space, in between, is called Turiyavastha. This is a kind of Samadhi State. This is the point of real Yog. It simply indicates the state where the heart is completely desirefree. This space is so short that it remains beyond the grasp of a person."

In 'Ram Charit Manas', the dream which Trijata, describes before Sita and others is the realisaion of this Turiyavastha. This state is not unreal like the dream it is true. Trijata is a living form of RITAMBHARA PRAGYA (ऋतम्भरा प्रज्ञा). The realisations of such a person are always true.

Swami Vivekanand says:

"The first principle, in the initial stage of Sadhana is that every knowledge comes through realisations. The fact, beyond senses should be deemed real, only after it's realisation. Our mind works on three levels - subconscious, conscious and super conscious. Only the Yogi, remains in the super conscious state. The realisations of that state are always extra ordinary and wonderful.

"Now, we want to know the truth under this consciousness. These realisations only lead to religious truth. The spiritual details will have to be collected through this state, we should also raise ourselves to that level, to which the realised ones had reached. If the same kind of realisations occur, they shall become facts for us. We can see and witness all that has been done and seen by others. A thing that happens under a particular candition, may happen again under the same. There is nothing unsure about it. It shall definitely happen."

Shri RAJNISH Says:

"This (Turiya) State Comes through meditation. The process of Dhyan, is the process of awakening the sleeping power inside. It may be named Kundalini, PRAN or anything. Much is asleep within us. Without its awakening, no achievement is possible. The power with which we live, is very surfacial. Inside there is great power, resting, sleeping, hoarded by us, untouched and will go waste with our death. It is like a person, having the key of his cash-box, but who deems a note of ten, kept in his pocket as his whole treasure, and starves himself foolishly. He may starve, feel thirsty and may beg, but is all the while ignorant of his wealth."

So far as the life is concerned, there shall be found such ignorant persons only. Few shall come to notice who make use of the wealth of their lives.

Swami Yogananda thirth, the writer of 'MAHA YOG VIGYAN'

thinks that it is wholly true that God power descends in the disciple through the Guru and with this God power, the knowledge of Maheshewar Yog comes to the disciple automatically. The Yogic reactions take place with this help. The sadhak becomes doubt free with his Own experience, with the words of his Guru and the shastras. The Kundalini power does itself what is necessary. Till the knowledge of the Sadhak does not embellesh and the Yogic reactions do not begin, the grace of the Guru is not established. He says further that the desciple is filled with knowledge and wisdom and happiness with the Shaktipat because that super consciousness is full of wisdom and happiness as a result of the wisdom and the happiness, the desciple has many Yogic reactions of the Hathyog and the mantras in the form of trembling, hair lifting and other reactions relating to the sound and the sight. These symptoms prove the might of the guide. The guide also feels assured by watching these reactions. The disciple feels the entering of a kind of power in his body. He feels the touch of electricity, inspiration and light also. Trembling, hair lifting, thrill, reactions in the eye, body and head and different reactions in the body like the head, begining to touch the earth, heavy breathing and very low breathing and breathlessness is felt. Some times the body feels as if ants were creaping over it. Drowsyness, deep sleep or unconsciousness like condition may exists. He feels like intoxicated one. The doubts and the alternatives dwindle or subside all together. A great feeling of activity appears along with happiness. He begins to react strangely also. Besides, he hears the Anhad Naad, sees divine lights, has visions of the Sidhas and the Gods and he begines to travel in the sky.

In some Sadhaks these things begin to occur instantly or after some days on account of the grace of the Guru or as deservings. Some undergo these reactions after a long practice. The power that is transferred by the guide to the disciple, helps in every kind of Yog Sadhana. That power is the super conscious power, The power of Shiv that comes to the disciple through the Guru tradition. That power is turned AGYA and it orders the disciple like a master orders his servant and gets every thing done.

According to a Yogic book, Maheshwar says to Parvati, "When the Kundalini of the disciple is awakened, and begins to interact, the mind, the Pran and the body of the disciple developes the symptoms of travelling etc. The Sanskaras of the millions of lives scatter into differet forms and the Sadhaka comes to know the knowledge of his previous births. It is not necessary that these interactions should start just from the time of initiaion, they may happen later on. The most difficult Aasnas, Pramayam, Mudras and other Yogic exercises begin to take place with quite ease. This Sahaj Yog delivers happiness and joy to the Sadhak beyond description.

The Yog Sadhana performed in the previous birth, develops further in this life after the in- comming of the Jagran Shakti. If the Sadhak tries to supress these activities, he feels uneasy but he enjoys himself in doing them. The Shakti Jagran is a passport to reach 'Turiyavastha'. With the help of this power the difficult path of Ashtang-Yog is easily crossed over. The Sadhak arrives at a high state of Samadhi.

Some Experiences and their Causes

CONCENTRATION (एकाग्रता) :-

Yog is a precious treasure of Bharat varsh. The composition of the Vedas, the Upnishads, the philosophies, the Geeta, religious scriptures, like Bhagwat and Puranas, the Volumes of Ayurved (Medicine) and Astrology etc., is the result of this wonderful Yog-Vidya. Yogabhyas, leads to Ritambhara Pragya, which reveals the truth easily. The veil of ignorance is removed and the knowledge begins to illuminate. As such the praise of Yog has been sung freely in the Sanskrit literature. The word Yog is associated with every chapter of the Geeta. The modern inventions of science by Newton, Marcony Einsteen, and Jagdeesh Chandra Basu etc. are the results of this wonderful power of concentration. No work of worldly or spiritualt importance has ever been done with out the concentrated mind. 'Yog' itself is the concentration of the Vrittis of the chitta. (योगश्चित वृत्ति निरोध), Therefore for treading the path of evolution and advancement concentration should be resorted to; otherwise the goal, worldly or other worldly, can never be attained.

The flow of the Vrittis of the Chitt, goes on ever unabated. If this flow is stopped with the grace of God for some time and one may become without Vrittis, it will open the entrance into the Yog marg.

Swami Ramananda says; "Concentration is unavoidable for the mounting of the super consciousness. The sadhana of the Aaroh path, is based on concentration but in the descendency of super consciousness, through the powers of Mantra or the guide, the Sadhak gets himself united with the SAHASRAR, meaning thereby that the current of the Maha Shakti begins to flow into him. When this current moves slow, the sadhak can not know it but some sadhaks feel clearly this movement into the SAHASRAR. We should know that the Mahashakti is the cause of all consciousness and this very Shakti lives in a man in the form of Atmshakti.

2. THE APPEARANCE OF POWER :-

Since the energy is conscious the appearances are of different kinds. When this energy interacts extraordinarily, the sadhak feels peace joy. His own vastness, the presence of divine powers, etc. This energy appears in the form of electricity, sound, light, word and speed. It also appears in the form of breathing through Pran. All these appearances are at the level of the Pran and Mind. The appearances of higher level are the outcome of higher consciousness. These appearances confirm the descent of power and its being activities.

Some, feel only a slight pressure over their heads, some feel peace descending upon them. Some feel themsalves placed under strange conditions never felt before. Some Sadhaks are prepared for them already and they start feeling these appearances very soon. Others take a long time in reaching that state.

The currents of energy come from above to downwards and they influence the centres below. These centres, on their turn radiate the waves of power towards the SAHASRAR to balance them.

In this way, the relay of the power-waves continues. The waves of power going downwards indicate the descent of power and the waves going upwards indicate the ascent. Some times, there s a conflict in their speed which the sadhak can feel himself. The movements from both sides are continuous and all the centres are controlled by the SAHASRAR, When consciousness stays in Sahasrar, the state of peace, stillness and the feeling of being witness (साक्षी) takes place. It seems as if nothing is being done by the sadhak. He is only an on looker under this state. The restrcuring of the personality of the sadhak begins. The nerve-centres of the lower strata posess the vritise of lust, Anger, Love, Hate, and envy etc. These vrities fail to grow stronger on account of the descent of the power from'above when the ascent of the power begins from these lower centres, these desires grow stronger enough at first to make the sadhak terrified. He feels himself dragged and degenerated. But if these are watched patiently, the conditions change. The instructions of the Mahashakti from inside must be heard and followed properly. If the sadhak is ready to give up his passions and desives and is ready to follow the guidance of the mother, he gets the guidance soon. To him, the instructions of the mother should be supreme. His submission to the mother may provide him with a chance to act freely leading him to the consumation of his sadhana.

THE MEANING OF APPEARANCES :-

The sadhaks treading this path, have different kinds of appearances. They occur differently to each Sadhak according to his state. These appearances convince the sadhak that he is advancing satisfactorily on the path of sadhana. Some of the appearances are full of consciousness; some are full of power and still others, full of different things.

APPEARANCES OF CONSCIOUSNESS :-

The appearance of consciousness have sphere of peace, They give joy and knowledge that opens the great secrets before the sadhak. It seems as if the waves of knowledge were rolling over towards him. He also fells that his existance has risen above the levels of mind and intellect. He witnesses everything like an on looker. He feels that the interactions in the Sahasrar give him peace and disinterestedness. The descent of knowledge becomes active in the state of the samadhi chetana of the power. The feeling of joy denotes the development of the heart centre. When the mounting up of power takes place into the heart for the first time; a very strange feeling of carefreeness appears in him.

When the upper centres are energised, the sadhak feels contented to have achieved everything. But after sometime, he finds himself into the lowest state. This cycle goes on till some special state is reached.

Sometimes there is a great intellectual activity in them. He becomes overwhelmed under the waves of joy. He feels himself rid of envey, jealousy, lust and anger etc. He feels himself full of peace, pleasure and power. He becomes fearless and self confident. He grows healthy and eager to do something praise worthy. It depends on the internal state and the sincerety of sadhana how long this state should continue. If the sadhak continues the sadhana with Niyam and Nistha (Faith), this state may continue for long. Otherwise, he may undergo a change. He may think where his inspiration and carefreeness has gone? These ups and downs continue till the state of total purity is reached.

Sometimes, some hetrogeneous elements start to come out. The supressed diseases errupt and then subside also. There is an increase of passions and of anger. These should not terrify the sadhak. He should go on watching and performing his sadhana. These erruptions subside slowly. This circle of peace and conflict, hope and hopelessness, success and failure goes on for some time. The erruption of these is a sign of the forth coming purification like the peace before the stom.

The experiences of power

Speed, light, electricity and word (sound), are the main appearances of this sphere. Speed: The crawlings of ants our the body, the movement of the nerves, the lightness of the body, lifting up of the ASANA from the earth, heaviness of the body, the bending of any organ of the body specially the neck, feeling shocks and jerks, at the time of sitting, are source of the main appearances of speed. The lightness of body indicates the development of of soul power (आत्मशक्ति) The heaviness of the body shows the pouring in of Mahashakti. The crawling of ants reveals the movement of power and the stirring in some part of the body indicates the affect of power on that particular part. Shocks are feel when the mounting up power collides with some obstruction. During such condition, the body should be relaxed fully and allow the power to interact freely.

ELECTRICITY : The currents of electricity seem to run into the head and other parts of the body. Sometimes the whole body is electrified. This feeling arises out of the interplay of the power.

The purpose of the electrifications is to eleanse the course of flow. It is a good symptom. The electric currents, washup the body and make it full of energy.

When the Muladhar is energised soundly the whole nerve structure is shaken. This is a good sign of the SHAKTI JAGRAN. It is advisable to inform the guide, if trainbling persists.

UPLIFTING OF HAIR (रोमांच)

When the Shakti becomes active at the heart centre, the thrill lifts up hair and causes a flow of tears.

Word (Sound) Based experiences

The subttle sounds are called Anahat which means that they come out without any clash. These sounds become audible due to the working of the power at different levels with their help, the inter action of the power becomes fast. These sounds come from the cosmos. They are without beginning or end like God, They are beyond the unit of Time and space. They are a modulated form of the Divine power.

LIGHT (based)

Sometimes the sadhak feels that lightning has struck among the dark clouds: Sometimes the display of clear moonlight takes place. Sparks and the lights of glow worms also appear lights of different colours, even like those of the sun, became visible. Light is a four of energy which is produced in the intence state. This light shawl the vision of God, through the eyes. It should be given a great reverence and regard of gratefulness.

VISITATIONS :

Almost all the sadhak feel that they have been transported to some alin land. They watch the scenes there and visit different places. They feel going upwards, then, enterning their physical bodies. They meet with such divine persons, sidhas saints and relatives who have left their bodies. Some reach the peaks of the Himalayas and meet and talk with the sidhas and seek their blessings. Some feel that the SHAKTI takes them to visit the distant spheres and leaves them back in their homelands. All this happens due to the expanding power. In the astral sphere, they meet the spirits inhabting there. Those spirits introdree them to their fellow spirits. This experience is an indication of the inner growth.

SIDHAS AND THE VISIONS OF THE GODS

The sadhaks during their meditation see sidhas with haired or shaven headed forms. Sometimes they have the visions of gods, quite unknown to them. These things need elaborate explanation.

SIDDHAS

The Sidhas that live in astral bodies, are beings that take interest in the sadhana of the sadhaks. They appear, and help the sadhaks in attaining a higher stage of their sadhana. The sidhas are capable enough to transform themselves into any human form or body according to their desire and need. Their duty is to help guide the sadhaks in their jorney of sadhana.

The ordinary beings have a limited bodyform, but the sidhas

have unlimited exterior. The life span of the living beings is limited and their bodies decay but the subtle bodied sidha's life span is not time bound and it may live for thousands of years. Some Sidhas live beyond milaniums. They exist in subtle forms and can assume form when needed, by their desire only. They are Yogis of very high order. They have the power to visit distant spheres (लोक) like NARAD.

These Sidhas can reach the sky in moments. Some Sidhas are still supposed to reside in the caves on the high peaks of the Himalayas in their astral forms. They perform penances and appear into body form for the good of the humanity. They have contact with the people and can make themselves seen and talked. They are always in search of the sadhaks with pure hearts and when they come across one, they help him devoutedly. They remove their doubts and misgivings and impart knowledge of higher kinds. They benefit the sadhaks with their own experiences. They are a sort of spiritual guides who are even in search of spiritual disciples.

The Sidhas are incorporeal beings but they need a physical body for their activities. The sadhaks live in physical bodies but they need abstract powers. Both are complementary to each other. The Sidhas feel elated by Camming into contact of the sadhaks; similarly the sadhaks feel proud of possessing the grace of the great SIDHAS.

If the sadhak is a pure being, the Sidhas come to him through his charms. They introduce themselves, create faith in the Sadhak and give him spiritual knowledge. The sadhaks should develop in them the virtues that are most liked by the Sidhas. The sadhak has to be simple, blameless, pious and benefector of all, besides having sincere devotion belief and faith in God. The unvirtuous persons can not even have a vision of the Sidhas. The sadhak crosses over successfully the hard way of sadhana, with the help of the Sidhas.

THE GODS :

The gods are the celestial beings inpregnant with Godly attributes. The have the respensibility of keeping up a balance in the universe. They hold charge of different departments and works of the creation. Different gods are the deites of a particular part of body. There are different details for different kinds of nature. They act according to the commands of God and remove the obstacles coming in the way of the sadhaks. They are like the offices on special duty, in the Divine governance. They protect the religious and destroy the irreligious ones. They rain their favours on the sadhaks incessantly.

These divenities extend their support without beeing asked for. Their relationship with the living beings is like the relation of PRAN with the human body. They goto the sadhak by themselves and provide him with guidance and support.

Part Two
SIDDHA KHAND

Saint Gyaneshwar

The name of Maharaj Gyaneshwar stands supermost among the saints of Mahrashtra. He was a great knower, perfect yogi and a prolific writer. He was born in 1352 Vikramiya to one Bithal Pant who was blessed that God himself will incarnate as his son.

Gyaneshwar maharaj is very popular for his miracles. He could make buffalo, utter the pious hyms of the Vedas; he could make the spirits of the forefathers appear in bodyform to accept the offerings at the time of Shraddha (श्राद्ध). His greatest miracle is to have written Gyaneshwari, at the age of 16. On the Bhawatgeeta. Gyaneshawari, published seven hundred years ago, enjoys the same repultion as the Ramayana of Tulsidas does today. He left wonderful statements about yog and Sadhana the result of his own experience and realization.

He asserts about Sadhana:

"A suitable place should be selected for yog practice while one should sit on an asian and concentrate on the feet of the guru. During the sitting one would feel that the body is becoming canditioned and that the Vayu is concentrating on one point. As one enters this state he crosses one point. As one enters this state he crosses over the nature. The posture of sitting should be that the lower parts of the feet should be upwards on the bent knees and they should be placed under the anus and pressed. This posture is called mool-bath or Bajrasan. When the pressure of the anus and the penis falls on the plexus between them, the upon vayu (अपानवायु) inside begins to go downwards. If the three bandhas occur together, the yog is thought to have started.

JALANDHAR BANDH

In, 'Jalandhar Bandh' the shoulders remain somewhat upraised, the spine erect and the head tilting down on the breast. The eyes seem sleepy, the upper lids closed. The eyes remain partly open, the vision fixed at the forepoint of the nrose. The sight can not go out due to the internal concentration and virtually without any desire to look out. The head bent down the chin touching the throat pit. This kind of state is called Jalandhar Bandh.

UDDIYAN BANDHA (उडीयान बंध)

Uddiyan Bandh, the nave raises itself up a bit and the stomach thrust insides becomes level. As such the bandh between the 'Mool Bandh' and below the name is called Uddiyan Bandh. This bandh is useful in eliminating the source and basis of desires. The power of imaging dries up and all the emotions subside. Even the hunger and thirst do not bother.

Mool Bandh (मूल बंध)

The Moolbandh, already stated above blows back the Apan Vayu which becomes furious and produces thundering sounds. It pressurises the Manipur Chakra at the nave. Before subsides, however, it flushes off the total mal (dirt) deposited inside the body. The wave of this Apana Vayu enters the inner cells and takes off the 'Kaf and pitta' from the hidden places. It transforms the 'Sapta Dhatus by purifying them. The beginners in the yog system feel terrified in the initial stage and they should not feel afraid at all. Though some uneasiness may be caused through this process but does immense good. This occurrences and the heat of the, 'Apan' energises the Kundalini also.

KUNDALINI JAGRAN

The Kundalini Nadi lies sleeping in the three folds with its head bent down, like the young one of a she Cobra, Kumkum red in Colour. It lies, bound soundly in the tiny place Moola Dhar, with the golden cords of electricity, brilliant like the flame of gold. But this sleeping Kundalini wakes up when it receives the thrust of the Bajrasan. It breaks up its bounds like the seedgerm breaks up its cover and comesout forcefully like a broken meteor. It stands upright and vibrates the whole body. It spares no part of the body. It inhales even the breath that goes out of the nostrils upto a length of twelve angulas. The Apan Vaya also raises upwards and the Pran Vayan also raises upwards and the Pran Vayan thrusts downwards. Between the time, there remains only the layers of the middle Chakra. If they could succeed in joining each other, havoc maybe created. However, they eat up all the earth and water element of the body and feel satisfied. Having satisfied themselves to some extent, they reach the Sushamna. They enter the Sushmana and break up the three knots of Bramha, Vishnu, and Rudra besides the six Chakras. The whole body is transformed then. All the parts become pure and divine. The intellect loses its vacillations. In the meantime, the pond of nectar stands upturned like the seventeenth day moon slowly and slowly, it turns down and touches the mouth of Kundalini, Then, the nectar, dipping out of the mouth of kundalini is absorbed in the whole of the body alongwith the Pran Vayu and finally dries up there.

Explaining this state, Lord Krishna says to Arjun that the body of the yogi, seems to be bright like gold externally but in weight as light as the air. The reason for this is that it is with out any earth or water content. Under such state yogi becomes capable of seeing things beyond the seas also. He hears the celetral sounds and can know the intent of an ant as well. He rides the horse of the wind and can walk over water without damping his feet . He enjoys many Sidhis of this kind. Therefore Arjun, give-up looking here and there. Make a strong ladder of Pranvayu and heart cells with Sushumna. That will take you to the heart. Kundalini is the mother of the world. When it enters the heart cave the divine Anahat Nad is produced automatically. The human intellect works consciously due to this Kundalini power only.''

The Anahat NAD (sound cosmic)

This sound is of ten kinds. The first is Ghosh (घोष) which takes the force of word figure Onkar (ओंकार). Unless the Pran Vayu is destroyed, there is noise in the heart sky, and the same keeps resounding. When Anahat Nad fills the heart like the sky filled with the thundering of the clouds, the window of the Brahmarandhra opens by itself. The Hrahada Kash, or Brahmarandhra, situated above the heart sky, contains consciousness also. As soon as the kundalini enters that Hahadakash, it provides it's energy (Tej) as food to the consciousness. When this pure food is used with the intellect, the feeling of quality disappears at once. It appears that it was covered with the yellow apron. This supper state does not need any Dhyan or effort. It is beyond the touch of elements and desires.

The result

When the Shakti has performed its reactions, the form of the body vanishes. The yogi, living in that state does not appear to be so in the eyes of the world originally and outwardly, he seems like a human being in body form, but in reality, his whole body remains composed of the element of air only. In that state he becomes Khechar, a being who can soar up into the sky. When the yogi attains this state he can wright wonders. When this yogi, walks, all the eight sidhis i.e. Anaima (आणियत) etc. follow him with folded hands.

Oneness of Brahma & Jeeva

When this (Kundalini) power settles down into the Brahmarandhra

(ब्रहांध्र) the Soham (सोहम) spirit unites with the Param Brahma Shakti. The cover of the five mahabutas shatters and the two powers unit together, assimilating each other into one.

As the sea water, purified by the cloud form, passes through the rivers and streams and ultimately unites with the sea, Similarly the soul (जीवात्मा) also takes the help of the body in Uniting with God. After the Union no thought remains that the two have become one. Similarly the dissolution into the sky, leads man to proper knowledge. All these things are beyond the description through the words.

Shri Ramkrishna Pramhans

Mahatma Gandhi, in the preamble of the book, Shri Ram Krishna Lilamrit, has stated:

The biography of Shri Ramkrishna Dev, is a testament of practical religion. It gives us the strength of seeing God, face to face. He was a living idol of God. His speeches are not the orations of a learned man only, they are the pages of his life book. He has expressed his experiences through them. For this reason, the impact that falls on the readers mind is indelible.

The character and behaviour of Shri Ramkrishna, is a lesson in Ahimsa clearly. His love is not limited to any geographical bound or any other border. My wish is that his divine love may inspire, all the readers of this biography''

.Sh. Ram Krishna Pramhans was born on 18th Feb, 1836. His name in childhood was Gadadhar. He was as active and playful in his childhood, as he was naughty and handsome also, His small body was full of unlimited expanse and unending seriousness.

He started being 'Bhavavishta' since the age of six. Oneday he saw the deep dark clouds in the sky and became unconscious (भावाविष्ठ) by seeing a crane flying there. This was his first communion with God. Since his childhood, he was interested in music and poetry. He loved in playing and acting with the idol makers and other children of his own age. Sometimes he astounded great learned ones with his erudition and speech.

In 1856, after the death of his elder brother Ram Kumar, he had to shoulder the responsibility of the worshipper of KALI TEMPLE. He was only twenty then. His divine life started since then and continued to grow upto the last. His experiences are a source of inspiration to the aspirants everywhere.

HIS DIVINE LIFE AND ACTIONS

The readings of his life through 'BHRAGU SANHITA', say that:

''The Native shall be religious, respected and engaged in virtuous deeds. He shall proclaim and establish a new religious order and shall be worshipped in the form of an incarnation of God.''

The wonderful experiences of childhood

The life of the childhood of Shri Ram Krishna Parmhans has been full of strange experiences. One day, he was going to visit the temple of Devi, along with some women, reciting the Devi- Songs, joyfully, he slipped into Bhav Samadhi. Tears started flowing from his eyes and he fell down on the earth unconscious.

One day, on the insistence of his fellows he acted the part of Shiv. He appeared like living Shiv. After speaking some words he debed into deep Samdhi. The play had to be stopped.

Whenever, he remembered and meditated on some god, he went into Bhav samadhi instantly. When asked, he admitted of having seen the vision of the respective god. This Bhavsamadhi had started as early as at the age of ten.

The experience of the Mounting Energy.

Shri Ramkrishna used to say that the letters of the mantras, pronounced at the time of Anganyas or Karanyas, appeared visibly on his body. Similarly he felt clearly the upward movement of the Kundalini, to whatever Chakra, it reached.

Merging into the sea of light

Once Shri Ram Krishna was singing devotionally before JAGDAMBA (KALI). He prayed earnestly and humbly. The experience undergone by him at that time, has been described by him thus:-

"The house, the temple, everything disappeared suddenly and nothing was left discernible. Only an unlimited endless, ocean of living light remained. Wherever, he looked, he saw the bright mains thundering and rolling over him as if to immerge[2] him completely.

Instantly, they took him, dashed against his body and thrust him into writtheir water somewhere. He felt nervous and became unconscious after receiving the blows for sometime"

The eagerness and the Darshan

After this vision of the ocean of light, he started crying impatiently and everytime for the Darshan of the World Mother. He had a great turmoil with-in him. Feeling great pangs of separation, he fell down and rolled on the earth, making great wailings and saying, "O, mother! Have mercy! Appear before me!" He cried and he moaned in such a way that a crowed collected around him Nobody thought of what the people would think and say of him. Ramkrishna said that the people standing around him seemed like shadows only. So, he did not feel any shy or hesitation.

He became unconscious duc to excrutiating pain. In that state of mind and heart, he saw the vision of the MOTHER. It appeared as if the mother were smiling, speaking and consoling him in various ways. She advised him also.

Once Shri Ramkrishna was taking a walk in JHAOTALA. Mathur Babu felt that JAGDAMBA was passing by when he turned back, it seemed that SHIVJI was coming. He rushed to Shri Ramkrishna, fell on his feet, and told him everything.

Mathur babu, insisted time and again that he might experience Bhav Samadhi. Once it occurred also to him. His condition remained upset for three days. He lost every interest in the world. Then he prayed to Sh. Ramkrishna to withdraw the state and to enjoy it by himself alone. Sh. Ramkrishna placed his hand on his chest and then only he regained his original State.

PRAYER FOR THE AWAKENING OF KUNDALINI

Sh. Ramkrishna Paramhansa, prays to the Mother vehemently:

"Wakeup, O! Mother, Kundalini! How many days have past asleep in Muladhar. Mount up towards the head for the fulfilment of the mission Shiva adores the SAHASRADAL KAMAL. O Mother! O, conscious energy, cross over the Chakras and eradicate completely, the sadness and grief."

Shad Chakras

When the six Chakras are crossed over, the 'JIWATMA' unites with God, casting off the kingdom of Maya. This union is called Ishwar Darshan. (ईश्वर दर्शन)

Seven Floors (भूमियां)

The seven stages, (floors) of Vedanta, some what resemble the six Chakras of Yog. The three floors of Vedanta, and the three Chakras i.e. Muladhar, Swadhistan and Manipur, the Guhyalings and the Nave are inhabited by the mind. When the mind rises to the fourth floor (Chakra Anahat) it seems as if the Jiwatma were ablaze like the flame of the fire. The Sadhak is completely wildered be this sight.

The flight to the fifth floor i.e. to the Vishudha Chakra, fills the mind with the desire of talking to God. The sixth floor and the Agya Chakra are similar. Ishwar Darshan is possible only when the mind reaches this floor. It is like the light of the lantern that can be seen but not touched due to the presence of glass in-between.

King JANAK revealed Brahma Gyan from the fifth floor or sometimes from the sixth.

The seven steps (floors) (भूमियां) are: Shubheksha 2 Vicharan 3 Tanumanasa 4 Satwapatti 5. Asansakti 6. Padarth Bhawani and 7 Turiyaga, followed by Mukti (liberation).

After the penetration of the six Chakras, there is a seventh Bhumi also. The mind is dissolved there. Jiwatma and Paramatma, become one. The condition of Samadhi persists. The feeling of body disappears. No external knowledge remains. The thoughts are eliminated.

"Without the Kundalini Jagran, consciousness never comes".

About Guru, (the spiritual guide), Ramkrishna Paramhans has written:

"God is real guru, if a sadhak seeks initiation (दीक्षा) from a human guru, it will not suffice if he is treated as a man. He will have to be treated as real God. Then only, there will be belief in the Mantra. The belief will cause everything to happen."

Sadhana in seclusion

It is better if the effort and practice of Sadhana is kept concealed and performed in seclusion. The Satoguni (the pure) meditate within the house, in some corner, in the forest and even sitting inside the mosquito net. At first the Sadhak should practice in Seclusion, secretly. Then only he shall be able to become like king Janak.

About the appearance of gods, he says that Kartik, Ganesh, Lakshmi, Sarswati are all present. They should be looked at! But Shiva, is always under Samadhi or seen dancing, reciting Ram Nam.

The symptom of Ishwar Darshan is when the Mahavayu comes from inside and advances roaring towards the head. Samadhi takes place then and Ishwar Darshan becomes possible.

Those who are learned only and devoid of Ishwar Bhakti their speech is always full of confusion.

Those who have realised God, find Him, in all the beings and the world. If the children are tended, the feeling of the tending God would come. The presence of God shall be seen the figures of the father and the mother. He shall serve them like God. After having realised God, the relationship wife and husband will dissolve. He will talk only spirituality. He shall live alongwith the memories of God and shall serve the Bhaktas. Since God is in all, they shall serve all.

Chaitanyadeva, when in his wordly coil recited Ram Nam with dance. When in half external state he danced with the Bhaktas. He went into

Samadhi as soon as he entered his internal self Sh. Ramkrishna used to say about him:

"He saw Gaurang in his full physical form with these eyes and not in vision, with his ordinary sight. Now he sees things in visions (Bhav Awastha) only.

"He had seen Gaurang in physical form. He had seen you and Balram as well."

The Result of Prayer

Sh. Ramkrishna said to the mother:

"Mother! I shall have no issues, but I wish that I should have with me a pure Bhakta boy always. Kindly give me such a boy. Rakhal came to him for this purpose. Those who are related spiritually have some part or quality in them."

"The mother made him realise in the temple that SHE is every thing. All is that. The idol is Chinmaya (चिन्मय) the alabastor is chinmaya. Inside the temple, I saw everyone drenched in Bliss. He saw the power inside, in the dazzling form. Therefore he fed the cat with the puris (पूड़ियां) of Her Bhog. Look! The mother is everyone even a cat. When she is reached, everything becomes visible in its reality. The nature of such a person becomes like the nature of a five-year old child. Dattatreya and Jad Bharat, were of this child like nature.

The waking up of the Kundalini with Bhakti

The Kundalini power awakens soon through Bhakti. God can not be realised without the Kundalini Jagran. The following verse should be recited with concentration, sitting in a lonely place:

जागो मां, कुलकुंडालिकी,
तू नित्यानंद स्वरूपिणी।
प्रसुप्त भुजगाकारा, आधार
पदम्न निवासिनी।।

"O, Kul Kundalini Mother! you are the embodiment of bliss. You sleep in the serpentine way in the Adhar Padma. Awake!"

When a sincere singing is made, Ish-darshan becomes possible.

A question arises whether the Sadhana should be done continuously.

The answer is, 'No'. In the beginning the sadhak should gird up his loins, but later on strong efforts are not needed. So long as there are waves, storms and deep turns in the river the sailor has to take the help of the sail (पतवार). After crossing over them, the danger also passes away. When the boat is out of the turns, and the atmosphere becomes favourable the sailor sits and rests while the boat drifts by its own. He simply keeps his hand placed on the sail. (पतवार) when the tempest of money and woman is past there is peace alone. When the fruit comes, the blossom fades. Similarly when God is realised, man does not have to act; neither he feels any interest in doing.

How to meet God?

None can see God with his physical eyes. By doing sadhana, the body and the sight and the throat become saturated with love. God is seen with those eyes and heard with those ears. This Love laiden heart remembers God with Soul. God does not appear without love. Full of love, God appears everywhere.

Shakti and God are one

Try and think millions of times, one can not go out of the sphere of Shakti unless he goes into Samadhi! I am meditating. I am contemplating'' all this thinking is within the realm of Shakti. As such Brahma and Shakti are impenetrable. If you know one, the other has to be known. They are like the fire and it's flame. The rays of the sun can not be invoked without invoking the sun. Kali is Brahma and Brahma is Kali. The difference is only of names. When she is inactive she is Brahma and when active becomes Kali.

The importance of the seven Bhumis (States)

There is a story in the VEDA, relating to these Sapta Bhumis. Mind moves into these Bhumis. When it is active in the world sphere, it influences the penis, the anus, and the Nave. It does not remain in the higher state then and is always after money and women. The fourth Bhumi of mind is the heart. It develops consciousness after reaching there and the presence of lights is felt all around. One is thrilled to see them and exclaims his wonders. He, then, does not turn towards the worldly wealth. The fifth Bhumi is the throat. The mind, arriving at this place, becomes completely free from ignorance.

He talks nothing but God. If one tries to talk about another matter, he goes away from that place.

The forehead is the sixth Bhumi of mind. Here it enjoys the vision of God day and might. Here at this stage also one has some fear. Charmed by the wonderful beauty, he wishes to touch and embrace it. But he can not do so, as is in the case of the lantern light put behind the glass. This

Bhumi, inspires Samadhi. The Brahma Gyani sees God. In that Bhumi, the body can not live for long. He remains unconscious also without food. If something is put into the month, it comes out at once. He breathes his last after living twenty one days in this condition. This is the state of Brahmagyanis. For others it is the path of Bhakti. After the visions (realisation) and on the instructions only, others can be instructed or initiated, otherwise not.

Sh. Ramkrishna has flalty uttered:

"Your temple is devoid of Madhava (God). You have filled it with the sound of the conch. There live eleven bats there night and day."

"There are some symptoms of Ishwar-Darshan. A light is seen, inner bliss is felt and the Mahavayu rises up creating the sound of Gur-Gur."

"After realisation some cast off their bodies. It is like the same as an idol of gold is cast in an earthen mould and the mould may be thrown or returned by the person."

"Woman is a magnet. Choose God as the greater magnet. Those who have realised God, do not look at women to induce fear in than. They look at the reality that women have some part of the mother and worship them in that form."

Becoming the Acharya

Those who have permission and have been given powers, can perform the difficult task of an acharya. One can not reach sublimation without the God. Guru. Those who did not have Ishwar Darshan did not get permission. Without the God power, none is able to liberate any being from the worldly bonds.

The Urge (प्रकार)

Some Bramagyani, asked Sh. Rama Krishan Paramhans, how God could be seem. The reply was:

By crying and bewailing for Him. People flow tears far their sons wives and wealth but no one weeps for God. So long as the child is busy with his toys, the mother keeps her-self engaged in the house errands. But when fed up with the toys the boy begins to cry bitterly, the mother then comes running leaving everything and takes him into her lap. God also does like the mother.

God is Sakar and Nirakar Both.

Sh. Ram Krishna has clearly stated:

"One who thinks himself the doer, can never feel the presence of

God in his heart. He is not only Nirakar but Sakar also. He gives Darshan. His darshan is possible with. Bhav, and Bhakti. The Mother appears in different forms. Yesterday the mother talked with me; she was putting on vermillion and coloured clothes.

He saw the mother into different forms. Oneday the mother came to me in the form of a Muslim girl. She had a Tilak on the forehead but no clothes on the body. A girl of six or seven years wandered, talked and cajoled with me."

While at the house of Hirdaya, I saw Gaurang. He was wearing black bordered Dhoti.

"The mother came to me in the form of the mother of RATI and asked me live in Bhav (भाव) I also told the same to Haldhari."

"Sometimes I had emotional possessions. At that time, my heart did not pacify till I had worshipped."

"I am the instrument and He, the player. I do, as I am made to do. Whatever is said to me, I repeat the same."

God's Childlike Nature

The realisation or Ishwar Darshan, makes the nature of man like a child. The power that is thought of is begot by the aspirant. God, just like a child builds a small structure, then destroys it, Playfully. So God also creates, sustains and destroys. The child is not in the control of the Gunas, similarly God is also beyond Sat, Raj or Tam gunas.

When Union with God is complete, the speech stops. The realised ones do not have lust, anger at all like the burnt rope. The burnt rope has a form but when blown, is reduced to ashes. Those who realise God, go beyond Dharma and Karma."

"Do you know what is His form? He is like the bubbles arising out of water. Various forms emanate from the Mahakash or Chidakash. An incarnation is also a form. The Lila, done by the Incarnation is the play of the primordial force."

"There is no need of being learned and pedantic. God appears when called for vehemently. There is no need of amassing knowledge of different subjects for God realisation. The state of a realised person is that he sees God in everything even in the ants. When the death of someone takes place suddenly, the realised person feels that only the body has been destroyed. It is similar, seeing God or His incarnation. God, incarnates in every age, in the form of man."

Sh. Ram Krishna Param Hansa, always gave very appropriate answers to the questions asked by his followers. Some examples are:

Q. How does one feel in SAMADHI?

A. As the fish kept in a small pitcher. When left free into the Ganga, becomes of Ganga.

Q.Is there no ego left?

A. No but some of my ego subsists. A piece of gold reduced to the last particle, retains some parts of it. Similarly little ego remains. It is like the spark of a huge fire, flashing. The external feeling and knowledge goes away but a bit of ego (अहंकार) is left so that the taste of I and you, may continue. Sometimes the ego (Aham) is eliminated completely. It becomes jad-Samadhi then: That condition is hard to define. The figure of salt went to measure the ocean; it dissolved there. Who should then come to tell the depth of water?

A god realised person becomes speech-less, silent. He expresses himself only through gestures. Ramkrishna explains this through a story. The husband of a girl sits in a room. Her mates enquire about him. She nods and smiles and then becomes mum. Similarly the God realised person also keeps quiet.

Once Shri Ram Krishan enquired of Mahendra, ''Do you dream of me?

Mahendra, ''yes, many times.

Paramhans, ''Preachaig something?

Mahendra, (No answer)

Paramhans, ''whenever I instruct you, think that God is instructing you.''

In the beginning one has to visit shrines, has to wear rosary and follow the Niyyamas. But when Ishwar Darshan takes place, the external rituals become need-less slowly. It is sufficient to recite the name, to have His memory and to contemplate upon Him.

Initiation (Diksha)

Shri Ram Krishna was initiated by Totapuri. He made him meditate for three days. The idol of the MOTHER flashed before his eyes again and again. He could not free himself from name and form. He was at his wits end. Totapuri ji took a piece of glass and thrust it forcefully into his head and asked Sh. Ram Krishan to meditate there.'' Raise your mind up. If the form of mother appears, cut it off with the sword of knowledge.'' said Totapuriji. And he reached into Nirvikalpa samadhi. The guru left him alone, he found himself with out the movement of breath and the heart beat. His face was illuminated with divine lustre. The guru was overwhelmed with joy. He did some Kriyas and he came out of samadhi state. The guide and the disciple both felt highly blessed.

The Guru has the vision of the mother

Once, Totapuriji, the guru of Sh. Ram Krishan, developed stomach-ache. He wanted to kill himself by throwing himself into the Ganga. But was saved anyhow. The mother made him realise that nothing could happen without her wish. He found mother everywhere in the night. He forgot his pain of body. He sat himself near the Dhuni (fire). The whole night was spent in the Dhyan of the Mother. In the morning he spoke to Sh. Ramkrishna and admitted that his sickness was a blessing in disguise. Due to this, he was blessed with the Darshan of JAG DAMBA, He was quite ignorant that far. He asked Sh. Ramkrishna to seek the permission of his mother to let him go. In the morning both of them visited the temple of the mother and she seemed pleased to allow him to go.

Adwait Sadhana

After the departure of Totapuriji Ramkrishna kept him engaged in Adwait Sadhana for six months. He forgot every knowledge of day or night. He lived like a dead man. Flies entered his mouth and nose and he did not make any effort to flick them away. The grace of the MOTHER, brought a Mahatma there. He laboured hard to bring him to consciousness. After that he started taking one or two morsels of food. After sometime, the Mother asked him to be Bhav Mukhi (भावमुखी) for the good of the world and the people. He became extrovert slowly and slowly.

Sh. Ramkrishna has explained that in the dead state, the natural inclination of the mind became upturned into Nirvikalpa state. When in Samadhi the desire of coming down does not exist. But for the sake of the followers, he had to come down. This becomes possible with the force of wordly or physical desires like drinking water or meeting some person. When these desires occupy the mind for sometimes the conciousness comes down slowly. Sometimes it turns back to go up again in the middle of the coming down. It's movement is checked with the force of some other desire.

By living in his Adwait State, he came to the conclusion that the Adwait state is the consummate state of others means like Bhajan and worship etc. That is the last state. This state is attained by itself when one is perfectly full of love for God.

He told his students that every morning, the mother informed him of the progress of every aspirant and explained to him the cause of blockage also.

Darshan of Chaitanyadev

He had the Darshan of Chaitanya in Nav-Deep. He described the incident thus:

"When I started departing from Nav-Deep, he had that wonderful vision. Two boys, incredibly handsome, and never seen before, aged 13 or 14 having a hallow around their faces, ran towards him, flying very fast, down from the sky, with strached hands and faces full of smile. He screamed with joy to see that sight. In the meantime, the two reached into him, and pointing their forefingers towards him, disappeared into his body. Immediately, Sh. Ram Krishna entered samadhi state.

Darshan of Mohammed Saheb

Sh Ramkrishna observed the rituals of Muslim religion for three days. He followed the Muslim pattern of life in food, drink and behaviour. On the third day he had the vision of a divine being, with long beard and a resplendent face. After this his mind was fixed in Adwait Bhava.

Darshan of Christ

Living and worshipping like a Christian for three days he had the vision of Divine person who was very fair and shining and coming towards him. This happened while he was taking a walk under PANCHWATI. He recognised him just being an alien. He had large eyes, fleet nose, but without any loss in his grandeur of face. For a moment he pondered over his identity but soon his heart told him that he was Christ. That person embraced him and disappeared into his body. He had deep samadhi after that.

What is Samadhi?

When the mind becomes free from 'Vrittis' (thoughts), the state is called 'Nirvikalpa Samadhi'. Once Sh. Ramkrishna saw the green grass and thought it to be his body. Just then, two persons passed arrived and he thought that they had trod over his body. He felt pain and his body went red.

Once he forgot himself while watching the Ganga. Two sailors quarrelled and fought there. It seemed to him that his body was being beaten with sticks. Real scar of beating appeared on his back.

Whoever has entrusted himself to the Mother, is never allowed to go astray by Her. Sh. Ram Krishan said that no one can attain God, without being gentle. One day be asked the Mother: "Mother! Why have you befooled me?" Being a fool, is a Shame."

Just then, Ramkrishna saw a heap of refuge. The 'Mother pointed towards that and said that it was the knowledge. Will he like to take that. Sh. Ramkrishna replied in the negative and requested to bless him with the devotion of Her feet. They were all for him.

Sh. Ramkrishna was ever ready to do anything for his disciples. Narendra told that one day, he lay on his bed, and bolted the doors from inside. But his soul living inside, was taken away to Dakshineshwar Temple and after a discourse and advise, was brought back and left on the bed. Once he told Narendra, that he was ready to beg for him, on every door with a bag in hand. Really, the person who has entrusted himself fully to the Mother can not suffer.

Rakhal, His mental Offspring

Before, Rakhal came to him, one day he saw the Mother, entrusting him with a little boy, by placing him in his lap. The mother told him that the boy was his. Hearing this, he was thrilled and surprised. He asked the mother how that could be possible. The Mother laughed and said that it was not his real son. It was his mental offspring. Sh. Ramkrishna felt relived to hear this. Rakhal came to him after some days and he recognised him being the same boy. When Rakhal came, he lived like a boy of three or four years. He want to sleep while in his lap. He did not think of going home, or even keeping away from him, more than ten steps Sh. Ram Krishan also fed him with milk, butter and played with him also, often, he made the boy sit on his shoulders. The boy never felt any hesitation.

Bhairavi Brahmani

She arrived with the load of books etc. from a boat Sh. Ram Krishna understood at once, that she had come for him. He sent for her through Hirdaya. She also came to him without any querry, she told Sh. R.K. That the Mother had ordered her to meet three persons. She had already met with two persons. R.K. was the third.

Then they went into conversation like a mother and son. She always had a Shaligram Shila in her month. Once she took it out, worshipped it and then entered the Samadhi. Sh. R.K. felt possessed with the Bhav (भाव) of Ram, and started eating the Naivedya. After coming out of Samadhi state the Bhairavi felt happy that Sh. Ram appeared and accepted her Naivedya. After this she threw the Shaligram Shila into the Ganga. She regarded R.K. as the incarnation of Sh. Chaitanyadev and Nitya Nand. Mathur Babu, called an assembly of Pandits. Sh. R.K. also was there. The chief pandit said there are Nineteen symptoms in an incarnation of God. Sh. R.K. had all these in him. Sh. R.K. agreed.

Once R.K. said that a young Sanyasi, resembling him, often came out of his body and preached him. Whatever, was said by him (Sanyasi), the same was redelivered to him through Totapuriji and Bhairavi, Sh. R.K. had Ishwar Darshan often. Yet he doubted whether it was the delusion of his mind. He wanted to believe only if a certain thing happened. This kind of wish was always fulfilled.

The Mother, never fails to appoint great persons for helping and doing special deeds of good for the Sadhaks.

Success through TANTRIK MEANS

Sh. R.K. says, "There are Chiefly Sixty Four Tantrik Sadhanas and I was made to go through all by the Brahmani (ब्रहमणि भैरवी). They were so difficult that most of the sadhaks degenerate in their course. But with the grace of the Mother, I passed over all, successfully. While going through those sadhanas, I had the feeling of maternity in women in general."

The Tantrik sadhana can be very intricate and dangerous; it requires vigorous self control and the least deviation may cause any disaster. He writes about it:

Once Brahmani, the Tantrik guide of Sh. R.K., brought a woman to him and asked him to worship her like a goddess. After the worship, Brahmani benuded her and asked Sh. R.K. to perform Jap, by sitting in her lap. Sh. R.K. wept and prayed to Mother as to what she was making him to do. Immediately R.K. felt that something had entered his body. An incredible strength came to him. He sat into the lap of Brahmani. As soon as he started the Jap, he went into Samadhi.

He states that he never took more than three days accomplishing a Sadhna. He was always impatient for the result and did not feel contented unless achieved. He sat himself near the Mother obstinately and as a result of this he got his prize within three days.

Experience of Kundalini Jagran

Describing his Tantrik Sadhana, Sh. R.K. says:

"He watched that the energised Kundalini was mounting upwards and all the dull Kamal Chakras, bloomed and stretched up. He felt various wonderful experiences occurring to him. Sometimes he saw a man of his own age, full of light and lusture, going to each Kamal Chakra and making them more embellished and resplendent with the touch of his tongue."

Once while sitting in Sadhana, Vivekanand witnessed Shining triangle of light fully alive. When he spoke about it to Sh. R.K. he explained that it was the Brahma Yoni (ब्रह्मयोनि). He admitted that he had also seen it once and it seemed to deliver innumberable spaces (ब्रह्मांड) out of it.

The various sounds of the space in an unified form are resounding every moment. He saw it clearly. The Mother Jagdamba, seemed to him place in the female vagina.

By-passing the SIDDHIS

Sh. R.K. felt the appearance of the Eight sidhis like, Anima (अणिमा), during his Sadhana When he enquired the Mother, about their uses, the Mother said they were like the human excreta and are to be discarded off. After knowing this truth he ignored them like anything.

The appearance of Bearded Ram

Once a bearded hermit named JATADHARI came to him. He had an idol of Ram. The hermit always carried it with him and fondled with it like a boy. The idol also played, ran, smiled, and did everything as desired by the hermit. Sh. R.K. saw this miracle and thought it only a delusion at first. But when the things happened repeatedly, he had to convince himself. Oncc the idol showed eagerness enough to live with Sh. R.K. The hermit had a vision of Lord Ram. He went away leaving the idol with Sh. R.K.

In whatever form (भाव) Sh R.K. penanced, the saints of that Bhav, started visiting him in chain. The urge and the aspiration of the Sadhak, make the realisation of God, an easy thing. The urge in Sri R.K., has been described by him in his own words:

"While being impatient for the union of God, I rubbed my forehead on the ground so vigorously that the skin was scratched and the forehead became blood smeared. In the same way I forgot the sense of Dhyan, Bhajan, Prayer, invocation and the rising and setting of the sun even. When the gongs were struck in the temple in the evening at the time of Arti (आरती) my pain become excruciating. He bewailed that another day had gone waste. I could not have the Darshan of the Mother that day also. I fell down on the ground, and cried so vehemently that the people gathered around me and pitted my suffering with stomachache."

Worship of Hanuman

He performed his Sadhana for sometime assuming himself as Hanuman. He meditated on Hanuman so intensely that he forgot his own entity. During that period he clad and fed himself like Hanumanji. One day, he sat meditating in PANCHWATI. He saw a woman with a brilliant hallow. It radiated the whole place. She started towards him. In the meantime a monkey came and sat at her feet. Immediately he thought that she was SITAJI. He was just about to prostrate at her feet, then She entered into his body and disappeared.

Sh. R.K. asserted that when the Sadhak become pure internally by practising Tyag and SANYAM and controlling his senses, he becomes Guru himself.

In that state the rays emerging from his clean heart, never allow him to go astray. His mind manifested into a personal form and bade him to do the right thing only. One day he saw during meditation, that a Sanyasi came out of his body, having a red Trident (त्रिशूल). He asked R.K. to throw away all the thoughts of things from his heart and to recollect his Ishta. If he did not do so, he will thrust his trident into his body. He watched further that a figure, smymbolic of lustful feelings, came out of his body and that was killed by the young hermit with his red trident.

In the beginning of his Sadhana even, he had the visions of a young Sanyasi. Sh. R.K. sought his advice on all important matters.

Once while travelling to Kamarpukar, he felt that small children came out of his body. They were very charming. They started playing different games. After enjoying themselves in long playful activities they disappeared again into the body of Sh. R.K. Shri R.K. told this thing to Brahmani after a lapse of one and a half year without being surprised. She told calmly that Sh. R.K. was an incarnation of Nityanand and Chaitanya and the experience was normal.

Internal changes during Sadhana

During the Sadhna, many physical changes also take place in the body. His body had such a great heat and pain in his body that he used to lay in the water of the Ganga for hours. Brahmani garlanded him and put the lotion of Chandan on his body to cool. He felt great hunger in those days.

There was an idol in the temple in the meditative posture. He looked at that. As soon as he sat for meditation, he could listen to the sound of the joints closing up. It's rustling seemed as if some lock was being put on them. As long as he sat in meditation he did not have the strength even to move the body slightly. He was compelled to sit unmoved, forcibly by some power. When the meditation was over, he listened the rustling of the unlocking joints as he had done at the time of starting meditation.

In the start of the meditation, he saw points of light like the glowing of the glow worms. Sometimes, he felt that all the directions were aglow with light like the one seen under fogs. Sometimes a sea of light seemed flowing before him. It seemed so to him even on opening the eyes. He could not know what it was all. He could not ascertain whether it was good or bad sign. He simply cried and prayed to Mother to guide him.

Living Idol

Formerly Sh. R.K. felt life in the stone idol. But later on he did not see the idol but the living, conscious, forgiving Mother instead in flesh and blood. If he put his hand on her nose, it seemed to breathe. He could never see the reflection of Her body on the wall in the light of the lamp. While sitting in his room, he heard the Mother, mounting up the steps bearing anklets in her feet and making clinking sound. When he came out to ascertain, he actually saw Her mounting up the stairs. Sometimes he saw Her standing on the balcony of the room, with her hair dropping loose. Sometimes she looked towards the city of Calcutta or sometimes towards the Ganga.

Love Natural (अहैतुकी)

Natural or selfless love means that the emotions of love may be reciprocated or not, yet, it should continue. Sh. R.K. also sat in seclusion and kept bitterly calling, 'Narayan'. He lost external feelings during his weapings and found himself absorbed in Mahavayu.

Once he saw a large ocean rolling before him. He changed into a fish and felt moving joyfully in the splashing water of eternity. If the Sadhak advances further and further with the ripping sound of the ocean, he may reach consciousness divine: The Anahat sound also leads the Sadhak to its source Brahma. This state is called Parampad but it can not be reached so long as there is ego.

The one who has only heard about milk is ignorant; the one who has seen it, has knowledge of it and the one who has tasted it has realised it. Anahad Nad arises by itself. This is the sound of ONKAR (औंकार). This sound is audible to the Yogis only; not to the man of desires: The yogis know that one end of this sound is in the name and the other in Brahma.

Shri. R.K. stated later on that he did not see the Chinmay form of God. He finds Him as the concrete (living) form. It was his habit to touch, embrace and see Him in human form. Now, God said to him that he has incarnated as man and should enjoy himself on the company of man. Sh. R.K. should live like a maid. The maid calls the master's house as her yet she knows well that it is not her house. Her house stands at the village.

He says:

The people can reach God, by being gentle. The effect of preaching is sure and certain on the gentle-minds. The ploughed land does not require stone pieces. The seed grows into the plant soon. The fruit also comes early.

When a bird becomes tired of flying high, it alights down on the branches to rest and recoup. In the same way Nirakar Sadhana is followed by SAKAR.

The Kinds of Samadhi

The Darshan of God, means reaching the Samadhi state this state is of five kinds.

1. The speed of ants. Mahavayu soars up slowly with the speed of an ant.
2. The speed of fish - Deep Diving.
3. The oblique speed - Standing.
4. The bird speed - Flying with spread wings.
5. The monkey speed - jumping from branch to branch.

There are two more kinds of Samadhis:-

One in which the Samadhi state is retained for a long time, even upto many days. This is called firm (स्थित) समाधि. The other is called UNMAN (उन्मना) in which the mind settles into the meditation suddenly and effortlessly. He says.

"During the state of Sadhana I saw that a man kept sitting beside me with a trident in his hand. Sometimes the Mother transformed me where the mind could enjoy the pranks of God and sometimes it ascended to the state of sublimity."

"I had wonderful experiences during the Sadhana. He united with the soul clearly. A man resembling him entered his body and he started enjoying every Padam Chakra. The closed Padamas rose up and bloomed fully with his touch. All the Padamas opened fully and he clearly saw that the drooping down Padamas turned their faces upwards."

"Sometimes I meditated assuring myself like the flame of the lamp. The flame remains still in the absence of air; so I also tried to meditate likewise."

In the beginning of the Sadhana all the objects of the senses appear in various forms. He saw a great hoard of money. There was a Shawl, and Sandesh (sweets) in a plate. Two women were also present there. They were wearing nose rings (नथें). He asked mind, what did he like to have. The answer was in the negative. It wanted nothing but the mercy of the lotus feet of God.

Once, he was in meditation under a Bilwa tree. A sinful figure appeared and started tempting him. He was in the form of a fighting white man. He wanted to give money, honour, sensual joy etc. But Sh. R.K. called the Mother. He prayed to the Mother to kill him. That enchanting form of the Mother remained ever fresh in his memory. She danced with joy and the whole world also danced with Her.

At another occasion, Sh. R.K. saw that he was being taken away by a sanyasi. He entered a temple where he saw the Annapurna of gold. One day, Nagen and Haldhar were studying Adhyatma Ramayan in a temple. At that time he saw a river and a forest nearby. Sh. Ram and Laxman, with their underwears on, came to him. Once he saw the Chariot of Arjun near the Kothi (कोठी), and it was being driven by Lord Sh. Krishna.

A naked man, roamed with him and played and joked also with him. That figure had come out of his body and was like an idol of Paramhans boy. Sh. R.K. started that he had two desires in him. First, he wanted to become the king of Bhaktas. The second was that he should not become a saint with a clean and starved body due to hard penance (तप). Whenever, he developed some ego in him, he fell ill the next day.

Maya and Brahma

The Mother, made him see Mahamaya also. A small flame started expanding in the room and gradually it enveloped the whole space. Next, he was shown a great pond, covered with moss. A portion of the moss appeared and a little water became visible. But soon after, the whirling moss encovered the whole water. Water was the symbol of God and the moss was Maya. None can see God due to this Maya. Even if one sees a glimpse, the next moment Maya, envelops it.

Sh. R.K. claims to have seen God also. He saw that the Akhand Sachidanand, has been divided into two parts of a circle. In one portion, there were Sakar Bhaktas and in the other, was Narendra, sitting amid the strong red light, in meditation. Shri R.K. requested the Mother to enwrap him in Maya, else he would give up his body in Samadhi.

The one, who lives with us in his body, was known to his father. His father had dreamt Raghuvir, in Gaya once, assuring his father of coming to him in the the form of his son. So, Raghubir works behind his body. Had it not been so, he would have failed to enjoy the communion of the Bhaktas and the Bliss of God.

In the end, all the powers of Sh. R.K. were transferred into Narendra. The Guru and the Shishya became one forever.

Sh. R.K. passed away on 15th Aug, 1886.

Swami Vivekanand

Swami Vivekanand, known as Narendra Nath in his boyhood, became the best Shishya of Sh. Ram Krishna Paramhansa.

He was born in 1863 in a reputed Kayastha family of Calcutta. His father Durga Charan and mother Bhuwaneshwari, both were of religious bent.

Narendranath loved to meditate even in his boyhood. At the time of sleeping every night, he saw a hallow of light. When this circle drew nearer and nearer to him he felt as if he were going to drown in it.

While as a student he became a follower of Brahmasamaj. The study of the scriptures and books of various religions, developed in him the curiosity to learn the truth.

He was inspired to visit Shri Ram Krishna by sir Hasty, the English Principal of his College. He reached Dakshaneshwar to have the Darshan of Shri R.K. Shri R.K. asked him to sing a song and that pleased Sh. R.K. very much. He asked Narendranath to revisit him. He sang a song again at his next visit. The experience which he had after-words, has been described by him thus:

"I sang the song. After the close of the Song Shri R.K. took me to his room. He took his hands into his affectionately and shed tears. Then he spoke, "I have been waiting for you impatiently so long. You did not even think of me." He added further with folded hands," My Lord! I know you are Narayan Rishi of yore and have come on earth to wipe off the suffering of the people of the world. Then he fed with sweets with his hands and allowed me to go on the premise of visiting again."

"I went to Dakshineshwar again after a month. I entered his room. He was alone in meditation. Seeing me, he called affectionately to go to him. After some time he went into Bhavavesh. I saw him advancing towards me saying some thing and looking at me fixedly. He came and put his right foot on my body. In doing so something wonderful happened. I saw that the room and the things started moving fast and disappeared somewhere. I also saw that the whole world and my ego-self was also advancing fast for merging into the all devouring great void. I was afraid to see all this. It seemed that the loss of ego was noting but death. I became desperate and cried loudly asking him what he was doing. I have my father and mother living yet. Hearing this he laughed heartily and rubbing my chest agreed to stop that process. He said that there was no need of haste. Every thing would occur slowly. To my great wonder, his touch relieved me of all that phenomenon and I became aware of my body as before."

At the time of the next visit, Shri R.K. took Vivekanand into his room and entered Samadhi State. Shri R.K. himself narrated the event to his followers later on:

After this, I asked several questions from Narendra i.e who was he? Where did he come from? What was the purpose of his birth, and how long would be his stay on this earth? Narendra replied to these questions introvertedly. His replies tallied with whatever I had known and seen about him. It is forbidden to reveral all that. His statements atleast convinced me about the fact that whenever he would know of my reality, he would leave this world. He will give up his ghost through yogmarg. Narendra is realised Dhyanpurush, the purest of his endless realm."

Shri R.K. spoke about Narendra adding: "Inspite of being a follower of Gyanmarg, the heart of Vivekanand is full with the qualities of a Bhakta." Pointing towards his eyes, Shri R.K. said that the eyes, like those of Narendra, can not belong to a Gyani. His heart is full of Bhakti along with Gyan"

Whenever Shri R.K. saw Narendra coming at a distance, he went into Bhawavesh soon. When coming to his senses, he used to talk to him on religious matters. Sometimes, he expressed the desire of listening to the song of Narad and as soon as Narendra started singing he went into Samadhi instantly.

One day, they had a discourse on Advait philosophy and he explained to Narendra the oneness of Jiv and Brahama. Narendra heard everything peacefully but he did not seem to agree with it. He went to his friend Hazra and expressed his doubts to him. How could he believe in the statement of Shri R.K. that everything, i.e., the house, the utensils, tree, and all of us are God. Hazra showed his assent and both of them laughed on it. At that time Shri R.K. was in Bhawavesh. Hearing the laughter of the two, he came out and asked as to what they were talking about. He came to Narendra smiling and touched Narendra's body. He went into Samadhi State instantly. Narendra writes about it:

The touch of that day, transformed him wonderfully. Surprisingly he began to feel that there was nothing in space except God. Even after coming home, he continued to feel the same. What ever was seen by him, all seemed God to him. When he sat to dine, he felt that the server, the food, the utensils and he himself were God. This state continued for the whole day. Narendra's mother asked the cause of that condition, but he could not explain. His memory came back to him after some days and then he realised what had happened. It was a bit of knowledge of Advait Vigyan, experienced by him. He was convinced that everything written in the Shastras was true. After this incident he never retained a doubt about advait. His reverence for Shri R.K. became firmer further.

Narendra passed F.A. Exam. in 1881, and then devoted himself to the study of western philosophy. He came to the conclusion that the confusion created by different philosophies failed to help in God realisation. It's study could not even give the ability of recognising the truth beyond the intellect. He was very disgusted to understand this fact.

In 1884, before the result of B.A exam was out, his father died suddenly and the whole burden of the family fell upon him. The heart of Shri R.K. became very sad at the condition of Narendra. He acclaimed pitiously that a great burden had fallen on Narendra. It would he good, if he got some employment. When Narendra came to know of this, he felt very sad. He requested Shri R.K. not to speak these miserable words to anyone, for an insignificant person like him. The eyes of R.K. were filled with tears on hearing this. He told Naraien that he could beg for him by going door to door. How should he feel shame for asking for a job?

Narendra wandered for a job daily without any success. The summer passed and the rains set on. One day he was totally exhausted and was unable to walk even a step. Darkness prevailed before his eyes. He lay himself in the Verandah of some one. He lost count of time. After sometime he felt that the veil of sadness was getting off his mind. Some one was consoling him. His doubts subsided and felt happy. He developed strange strength in him and his tiredness was gone completely. He got up and reached home when it was going to dawn.

From that day he rose above praise and abuse of others. He realised that, he was not made only to earn and maintain his family. Having decided thus he started preparations for renouncing the would like his grandfather. He came to know that Shri R.K. was about to visit some Bhakta soon. He felt Satisfied that he shall pay the parting visit to his Master, and go into the unknown world for good. When Sh. R.K. came, he asked Narendra to accompany him to Dakshineshwar. He went with him and sat in his room. He became Bhavavishta soon. He got down from the seat (तखत), and putting his arms around the neck of Narendra started singing and weeping.

"कथा बलते डराई, ना बलते ओ, डराई।
(आभार) मने संदेह, बुझि तोभाग्य हराई, हा, राई।।"

"I am afraid to say and afraid not to say'
My heart is apprehensive that I may not lose you."

On hearing these words, Narendra's eyes became wet with tears. He was sure that R.K. had known everything. All the people present, felt surprised to see our condition. When one of the persons present asked for the reason, Shri R.K. laughingly said that it was nothing. Just it happened.

When all the people had left, Shri R.K. called Narendra to him in the night and said, "I know, you have come into the world for the work of Jagdamba. You will never stay in the world. However, you live in the world till I am here." Saying this, he started weaping again.

One day, Narendra sat meditating in his room for long, forgetting any regard of time. He continued to sit even after the meditation was over. Instantly, an image came out of the wall and stood before him. There was no expression of thought or worry on its face. It looked like a peaceful hermit with shaven head and having a Danda and Kamandal in his hand. The image looked at him for sometime. It seemed to say something to him. He developed a sense of fear in him. So, he got out of the room. He repented after wards. Perhaps that was the image of BUDDHA DEV.

While in Chicago Narendra had to deliver more than a dozen speeches every day. He had to think out, what new thing he should say. It seemed that his memory had disappeared some where suddenly. One day he went to bed after delivering a lecture. During his sleep, he heard some one deliver a lecture. In that speech, he heard about so many new things, that he could not have thought in the whole of his life. After getting up, he remembered that speech and delivered the same in the assembly.

In this way he heard many discourses, their exact number can not be given.

The modern psychologist will say that the ideas being in the subconscious mind appeared in his dream state or that the astral body was making the speech and the physical one was listening to it. It may also be possible that some un-manifested spirit was speaking for him. Anything may be passible but things do happen like these.

Once Swami Vivekanand went to visit Amarnath temple. He had the Darshan of BHAWANI at that time. The muslims had destroyed that temple. Swamiji started thinking about the incident. He heard clearly the mother saying that the temple was destroyed as per her will. She wished to live in that dilapidated temple. Had she wished to reside in a multistorey palace she would have got it built there. What Vivekanand could do for her? He could not protect her: on the other hand she would protect him. When swamiji heard this divine oracle, he gave up the idea of erecting temples etc.

One may doubt and say that the Oracle was the echo of his own thoughts. There is nothing outside. However, may it be voice of the heart or the echo of something outside, the hearer of such words, feels with-in himself talking to some one else. Sometimes he related spirits also deliver messages. They manifest into human forms and talk face to face and give distant information as well. Some pious spirits do help men through their words or even with their bodies.

Swamiji, narrates his experience of this type:

"One day, while at Kashipur, sitting in a garden he requested Gurudev and meditated by sitting beside him. It was a great pleasure. He forgot his body. The sun, the moon, directions, time and sky, all disappeared somewhere. He lost his wits and sense. When the sadhak concentrates on the thought of 'I' and 'Brahma' the two realities become discernable, indicative of duality. The state that he experienced that day, never occurred to him again when he told this to Guruji, he said that diving in that state day and night, could not be of any avail. Therefore he will not attain that state. However, he will be blessed with that state, when the will and act of Bhagwati is completed."

Such live experiences can not be overlooked only by saying that they are the hallucinations of the mind. Such experiences have been stated in the Vedas, 'Upanishads' and other shastras. The saints have described them in allegoric forms or symbolic languages. Even today, they are being experienced by the different sadhaks. One who realises the truth and reality, his attitude towards the life and the world undergoes a total change. The knot of his heart become loose and all the doubts Vanish. Swamiji says:

"Gurudev, called me alone, near him just before his death. He sat before me and started looking at me with concentrated mind. He became Samadhistha soon. I atonce saw that a circle of fast light emanated from his body and advanced towards me with the flash of the lightning. It dissolved itself into my body. After some time, I also lost the feel of my body. I did not know How long I remained in that state. When I regained my physical state, I saw Guruji, crying. He told me affectionately that he had given all that he had. I shall be redeemed only when I shall benefit the world with the help of this (her) power."

"I am sure, that power of, Gurudeva, makes me do every thing."

The Bhaktas inherit the spiritual treasures from the Guru, according to their deservings. The sad-guru is the ocean of spiritual knowledge but the disciple can only acquire the spiritual water according to his desire and Capacity.

Arvind Ghosh

Arvind is one of such great Yogis of India, whose lusture has not embellished only India, but also the whole world. He started feeling that he was sent on earth for some special purpose. He was born on 15th Aug. 1897 and breathed his last in 1950. A number of divine feelings and experiences, associated with him reveal that many unmanifested divine powers and God himself, lived with him. He got his education in England. He took part in the political movement of India, after returning here.

While a political prisioner at Alipur prision spiritual experiences with him started taking place. He admitted that the first lesson of spirituality was learnt by him in prison. He remembered that before one month of his arrest and jail, he had received inspiration to keep away from all kind of toils and troubles and go in seclusion to have communion with God. He had earlier realised that the whole visible world was pervaded with a spiritual power. He felt that the same power was spread in the whole sentient or insentient world. It was very kind and friendly to all (सुहृदं सर्वभूतानाम्). The world is it's living image.

After his release from the prision, he said at Uttar Pada: "I looked at the prisions separating me from other person and found that I was no more with-in the high walls of the prision. I was surrounded by, Basudev. (वसुदेव). I was taking a walk under the branches of the tree standing before my cell. The tree disappeared and I saw that Shri Krishna was there and was protecting me. I saw him in the cell and outside in the form of the wards. When I lay on the blankets, I feel that I was in the embrace of my associate Krishna. I saw the image of Lord Krishna even in the thieves, robbers, murderers and scoundrals, The prision became a temple to me where he could have the Darshan of Sakar Bhagwan."

He had by now, realised the existence of the unseen power of God. He attained Nirikalpa samadhi under the guidance of Yogi Lele.

He started the work of self writing, meaning that anything was got written by him by some unseen power. The pen was put into the hand the writing was done by some unseen power.

One day, he was directed to proceed to Chandra Nagar. This divine direction was received by him while sitting in the office of 'Karmyogi'. By now, he was accustomed to act at the divine directions. So, he left the office with out any hesitation. He crossed the Ganga, in ten minutes with the help of a friend and reached Chandra Nagar. He lived there everytime in Samadhi State. In Chandranagar, though his eyes were open yet he was at constant samadhi.

At Chandranagar, he used to have the visions of four divine powers. They appeared during the samadhi and stayed with him during the Samadhi. Shri Arvindo came to know the reality of those powers after reaching Pondicherry, they were all, Bharati, Mahi & Saraswati. The political leaders tried to drag him towards politics but he did not deviate from his Tapassya.

While at Pondicherry, he realised the secret of the mysterious Ved-Mantras that the life is struggle-field. This is the place of the struggle between the Devas and the Assuras. Different kinds of divine and natural powers of light and darkness are at constant war. Man is only an instrument. The divine powers try to free-him from the trouble of death and birth. This statement is not an allegory, not a figure of speech. This is the secret of worldly creation described in the vedas, a history, wrought at the hands of the divine powers. These activities are the expression of divine experiences and powers. They require extreme urge from downwards. God, above shall descend only then. All the Avataras have become a link of that animal evolution. The epitome is yet to be attained.

Shri Arvind received letters from many sadhaks containing their experiences. They wanted to know the real meaning of those. He replied to them accordingly. In an answer to a sadhak, he writes.

"The primary aim of Yog is to associate with this consciousness and to surrender one's nature to that light so that ones inner existence may unite with God. By doing so, one's nature shall turn into a playfield of divine, knowledge, power and pleasure" This is possible only when this wish becomes the sole goal of life, and all other things should be subordinated to that goal. This kind of determination, shall be a kind of preparation for the divine one. Explaining the truth of experiences he says that every appearance has some meaning. This power of experiencing shukshma darshan is vital for yogi and it should not be neglected. But the most important thing is the change in the consciousness. Other powers, like Suksmadarshan must be developed with out any attachment, regarding them as a part and help in Yog.

The visions of gods and goddesses do take place during meditation. The divine beings - gods and goddesses are the powers living above the world, and controlling the divine actions. Brahma, is that power of God, that lies behind the creation; Ganesh is the power of knowledge that removes all the hurdles. Kartikeya denotes the power of victory over other forces.

After reaching a certain state of mind the sadhaks not only have the darshan of the gods and the siddhas, they are made to visit divine spheres by them. The gods and sidhas talk to them, remove their doubts and inspire them to advance. They guide and escort them. The gods are said to be immortal and they are still alive as before though in astral body. The need is to seek their help through Sadhana. Replying to a Sadhak, Arvind writes:

"The people you saw with Lord Krishna they were just like humans in form. They talked and acted like ordinary human beings. The people living around do not know and regard the God. The boy, with the flute is none but Lord Krishna. He incarnated on earth from divine Anand Lok for his Lila. His flute is the invitation, the music to transform the ignorant Lila, into Anand Lila. It was your conscious being that heard that call and responded to it"

"The sight of the golden 'Om' ॐ rising in the sky indicates that endless chetana which has become replete with super-consciousness and is advancing towards Paratpar Chetana."

In his book, 'Yog Sadhan ke Pramukh Tatwa,' Sri Arvind writes: "Every man has the power of divine visions. But it remains concealed mostly. It appears suddenly in some persons of rare state. Those who have this power of darshan, retain this power on the external plane. It springs up with the first gentle thrust.

A sadhak wanted to know the secret of seeing rays of light coming out of the trees. He explained that they are always there. They are only concealed from the physical eye. A sadhak can witness those that are beyond ordniary sight.

All the advanced shadhaks see lights of different colours. Explaining the scheme of colours shri Arvind says the combined blue and golden indicates the presence of Krishna, and Durga Mahakali. The hallow around the face describes brilliance and divinity. The sadhak that are devoted to the super power fully, perceive the reality by themselves.

"The golden light ordinarily is a light or flash coming from supermental sphere. This is the flame of Satya Gyan. The Orange colour indicates the secret power. The white flame is the light of consciousness inside prana. The blue light is expressive of the super Mind. The star always hints at the coming divine light."

The sadhaks feel the rising and upward going of the power. The intensity of power is not bad provide it interacts for purifying the base or it brings with it, light, peace or ideas relating to higher consciousness. On the contrary if that power brings darkness or Rajsik Ahankar, Causing disturbance to the existence, it is a negative power.

When the mind become free from its obstructed path with the help of human conscinsness, his inside in filled with the awareness of the super consciousness. The sadhak beginas to understand the plan and purpose of the universal soul and the cosmic Bhagwati Chetna. He becomes a playfield of that power, Sri Arvind says:

"God is the source of light, knowledge and spiritual success. He is like the living Sun. Whatever man gets, he gets it from him. He feels everything coming from God. This kind of relationship with God is greater one than the relationship between the Guru and the Shishya."

The natural process of Dhyan is to develop the urge, The greater the prayer, the concentration the greater shall be the advancement of the Sadhak.

The Experiences of Divine Consciousness

When the Consciousness of the Sadhak awakens, he become like Shiva, with the third eye. In his ordinary physical body, he seems limited within his external chetna. But as soon as he goes beyond it, he begins to associate with the higher consciousness and can find the existense of spheres above. He can have contacts with the beings that abide there in unknown numbers and varieties.

The powers acquired during the Sadhna should not be treated as the sadhak's own. They should be accepted as the blessings of God. They should not be used for any personal misuse or purpose. It should always be kept in mind that he is only an instrument of God.

"Always live the life in a way as if you are constantly under the working eyes of God or the Mother. Never do anything, or think any thing that may be undeserving for the presence of Bhagwati Chetna."

Sri Arvind succeeded in bringing down the Superamental consciousmers into human body. He, not only told the way but got individual sidhi also and produced an example before us. He says:

"When one practises, a very high spiritual nature operates in him and he has to subordinate his individual nature to it. Though the lower one reacts adversely it is possible to enter the higher state of nature through sadhna."

He was associated with divine powers. According to him the centre of shuksma Darshan is in between the brows. When it opens with Sadhna, the sadhak begins to have darshan. He can look upto the difference between the things and the people. At the opening of this centre, the Yogic

Chetna becomes active. One can certainly develop the Shakshi-purush Chetna but if the lower nature is allowed to operate on it's own path, it shall not become Shakshi-Chetna. He did not believe that any emotion or baser nature, if allowed to manifest, will prove a means of getting rid of that. If one allows anger to find a vent anger will occur again and again and will become the master. Therefore the first act of getting riddance is to negate its expression. After that one would cast it off from ones thoughts and experiences. If one disowns the evil, one will have power to throw it off.

Peace, firm resolve and happiness should be confirmed with the memory of God. Never allow the clouds of evil thoughts to rain. Once allowed they shall force again and again. Reject them and they will disappear.

Only those things should be allowed to grow which are helpful in yog-sadhana. Develop your Capabilities which are helpful in the attainment of your goal.

The Condition of Sadhana is to live within, to be always full of Antar Chetna and Antar Anubhuti.

When the sadhak attains the State of Cosmic consciousness, he feels oneness with the individual soul.

Our Sadhna is based on the truth that the higher spheres and divine powers should come down and the lower Chetna should aspire to higher spheres. Then only there shall be a transformation in the individual nature of lower kind.

"Sadhna means the worship of God, to love God and to surrender oneself to God fully, to have an urge for him, to pray to him or to cause Nam Jap. Tapasya and Aradhana are also foms of worship."

"If one establishes contact with divine souls through worship, one can attain Godhood. The attributes of peace and detachment increase. The contact with divine powers helps a lot in Sadhana."

"The visions of lights coming repeatedly prove that the sadhak has gained the State of entering into Shukshma States. This power is dormant in every person and manifests only through Sadhna."

"Different kinds of lights are concerned with different powers. These lights come from higher Strata to lower one. The aim of this Yog is to have contact with Chetna first and to live in that light. It is possible only when all things are subordinated to this goal."

According to Sri Arvind, in the first stage of Sadhana, many shuskma darshan do take place. They are the creations of mental State. It is rather different to pinpoint their purpose, because they are based on the individual mind. But the later darshan shakti is very important for sadhna. The Sadhks should however, advance on their path of sadhana unabated.

Sri Arvind, with his successful Sadhna, had realised the sole truth, the knowledge of which reveals the secrets of all knowledge. He says:

"It is really a great achievement to learn what elements make the Sun or what are the lines of the Mars. But when you will get the instrument, with which you shall be able to see the human soul, just like a photograph, You will be in position to regard the achievements of Physics like the achievements of a child in play and you shall laugh over it."

Sri MÃ of Arvind Ashram

The mother was born in france in 1878. She met Arvind in 1914. The Ashramiates of Arvind called her, Mother, Shrimaa, or Divine mother. The whole Ashram was permeated by her.

An Ashramite Neerad Varan has written about mother:-

"The divine knowledge was reaching her since Childhood. She continuously felt that she is surrounded by a vast conscious power and had a hallow around her face. She started meditating at the age of seven, without understanding anything about Dhyan. Her chetna was not like that of an ordinary person. Since the young age, she realised that the purpose of her birth was a special one with some great responsibility to fulfil."

She always felt the presence of some superhuman power in her and seemed to enter her body and make her do wonderful things. Once, when ascending a hill she slipped and fell on the spearheaded stones below. But she felt that she was being taken in a lap and she stood upon her feet without having any injury.

She was taught through many Gurus in her young age, in day dreaming. She saw source of them later, alive. She got the acquaintance of Sri Arvind only through those gurus. She called them Krishna. She recognised Arvind at once when she saw Arvind in Pondichery. She held that France was the land of her birth and education but India is her soul.

She had a wonderful dream repeatedly at the age of 13, While sleeping, she felt soaring up in the sky with a golden garment fluttering around her. The agrieved men, women, old and young sheltered in it. The garment expanded upto them, like some sentient being she got rid of their sins and grief simply by touching that garment. This dream was very, vital to her. She felt universally happy by relieving the pain and suffering of others. The dream became a truth later. She redeemed the sins and pain of unnumberable persons in her life.

During the dream period an old man with crimsan coloured clothes. Kept standing beside her. She later understood that he was the unhappy man.

In her child or girlhood, when she visited the garden in Paris, she became one with the trees and the plants and knew their feelings. These experiences were written down by the mother in her diary, before coming to the Ashram of Arvind. It was a proof of her Spiritual progress. The aim and activities were just like Arvind. The same consciousness operated and acted into two body forms differently.

The whole life of the Mother is full of experiences. She had full awareness of internal power and evolution.

The initiation into Arvind yog, starts with the Darshan of Shrimaa and consumates into her knowledge, into her darshan and her possession. Sri Arvind says that every sadhak, without exception, shall acquire light and power through Srimaa only, never direct from him. She shall be the guide and preceptor of every sadhak.

The truth is that Srimaa, was ever established in super conscious state. In the beginning she was a human figure later she transformed herself into the status of divine mother.

Sri Arvind proceeded towards the super Conscious state through his Sadhana and it was his aim also. Long before her meeting with Arvind, Srimaa was already advancing towards the super conscious light. The exposition of the divine truth was taking place equally in the lives of both of them. The pages of her diary, written before her arrival to Pondichery coroborate this.

Sri Arvind has admitted himself that a common divine consciousness has possessed the bodies of the two for fulfilling the divine task. If such a divine power alighted on the earth, it may cause any wonderful thing to happen. In this connection, what Shri Arvind has written in his epic 'Savitri' is perfectly, true...

"यदि यह रमणी वही कि जिसका जग ने नाम सुना है।
तो आश्चर्य नहीं, कैसा भी मंगल घट सकता है।
उसमें अद्‌भुत एक रसायन की महिमा बसती है।
भरे हुए आश्चर्य, जहां ऐसी ही धरती है।।

"If this is the woman, whose name has been heard by the world, anything wonderful may happen through her. There lives a strange alchemy in her that is akin to the various jewels found in earth."

After the passing away of Sri Arvind, the Arvind ashtream was run as before by the Srimaa. She was a phantom of divine however. Her darshan only infused divinity in man. She appeared before the ashramites daily and regularly for darshan and distributed flowers of different colours to all. So long as the mother lived, the Ashram developed on and on. Her divine cohesiveness is still pervaded in the Arvind Ashram.

Param Hans Swami Yoganand

The world renowned Mahayogi Shri Yoganand, whose biography "Yogi Kathamrit," has caused a reawakening in the spiritual world, was born in 1893 in Gorakhpur. He was the disciple of Yogiraj Yukteshwar ji, the grand disciple of Lahire (लहिड़ी) Mahashaya a famous Yogi of Kashi. The biography written by Swami Yoganand is a wonderful book which describes the miracles caused by the superhuman powers possessed by them, through ordinary stories.

The system of spiritual practice adopted by him is called Kriyayog (क्रियायोग). The purpose of his Sadhana was to redeem the people from their physical elements, mental troubles and spiritual ignorance. He brought about a balance between the basic preambles of science and religion through personal realisation. He established spiritual unity between the East and the West and astounded them by acquainting with the immense treasure house of the spiritual knowledge and power of the Yogis and the Sidhas of India. He passed away in 1952 in California (America)

On account of the Sanskar's of his prebirth he had a great attraction for the Himalayas. He was always very eager to meet the Yogis and to avail of their communion. He declared in his biography that in his previous birth, he was a Yogi, penancing on the Himalayas. In his early childhood, he started showing the characteristics of a Yogi. He left his home in search of a Guru, without telling anything to anyone.

When a Sadhak is on fire to find his mentor he becomes impatient and restless. Under such situation, the Guru himself, inspired by some unknown power starts moving towards the Shishya himself. Otherwise the Shishya may find the Guru by his own efforts also. The same thing happened in the case of Yogan and. He writes:

"One morning, under a Satwik resolve caused by the hurt of his heart feelings, he entered his room and decided to keep sitting in meditation till he did not get a definite response or answer. Hours after hours, elapsed but there was no response to my humble prayer. Suddenly he felt that he had entered a void physically. In that endless void, he heard a divine and sweet voice of a woman, coming from some unknown direction saying": your Guru is coming today."

I washed my face, met with tears and obeyed the oracle humbly.

"While passing through a narrow lane of Varanasi at the corner. I sighted a Sanyasi in Vermillion clothes. My eyes became transfixed on him. Even then, I moved on. After ten minutes, my feet became numb. I was unable to walk. I turned backwards and stood there. The saint was attracting me towards him like magnet. I saw, his peaceful figure, gazing at me. After reaching him, I prostrated at his feet calling "Gurudev!" His was the face, I had dreamt several times.

"The Guru answered overwhelmingly and overjoyed in Bengali", O! my friend! You have, come to me! How long had I been waiting for you? My prostration at his feet now, was not the first one."

"Taking my hand into his, he took me to his cottage. Reaching there he said that he would give him the cottage and everything that he had got. I replied that I had gone only for knowledge and realisation of God."

"The Gurdev told me that he had given him his total selfless love and asked If I also could do the same. I promised to do so."

"Divine love is endless, boundless unconditional and unchanging. Even the touch of pure love, removes completely the flow of human desires from one's heart. I had, so long, told nothing to him about my life. Now, it all seemed unwanted. When I asked his name he said," Swami Sri Yukteshwar Giri. My head office (Ashram) Stands at Shri Rampur in Ramghat lane. You shall come to me in four weeks. When we meet again, you will have to arouse your interest in me. I shall not accept you as my disciples unless you agree to submit. Your soul fully in following the hard instructions."

"Bowing respectfully, I took leave of him. I took a count of 28 days after the meeting, and remembered that the Guru had asked me to meet after four weeks." I approached him. He welcomed me, sitting on the lion skinned seat. I touched his feet reverently. I said that I had surrendered myself fully to him by my own wish. He asked me to go to Calcutta and continue my education. He told that one day, I shall have to go to the west."

"The people of that place shall be more receptive towards the ancient knowledge of India, provided the Hindu teacher teaching them holds a university degree. I said that I would abide by every instruction only on the condition that you assure me of Baghwat Darshan. The guru assented and decided me to initiate into Kriyayog the next day. His very touch, seemed to cause a flow of fierce fire-light into body and my heart was filled with great delight."

"Yukteshwarji gave a gentle pat on my chest and my body became still. The breath went out of the lungs as if sucked by the force of magnet. The mind and the soul became free from the feel of inert body and started coming out it like a free flowing current. At that time the physical body became dead like yet I realised that I had never been in such a state before. The extent of my self now, did not limit itself to the narrow body, it seemed to permeate every atom. The people walking at a distance, seemed to walk into my wide circumference. The roots of the plants and the trees appeared clearly to me. Not only this, I was appeased looking at the flow of various 'Rasas' into me as well.''

''Everything around me, was visible to me clearly. My physical sight limited to the things standing before, transformed into a circular gaze that could look all around. I could see people walking in the Ramghat lane, behind the head. I saw a white cow emerging into my sight and when it reached the open gate of the ashram, I saw it with my physical eyes also. I could continue seeing her, even if it had moved forward. My soul was inundated with gladness. I realised that God was an endless ocean of joy. His body is made up of innumberable light cords. The light expanding within me, engulfed the earth, the continents, the sun and the stars. The whole space seemed to illumine inside me. A strong light was on me, providing me with unending happiness. The divine rays radiated out of the eternal source''

''I listened to the countless Pranav-Dhwani (प्रणवध्वनि) clearly. Suddenly my breath returned to the lungs. I found that my unlimited vastness has gone. I found myself caged again into my painful body.

''My mentor stood beside me during while all this happened. He had provided me with the bliss of experiencing the long-sought divine consciousness i.e. Samadhi. I prostrated myself at his feet to express my gratitude but he helped me to stand erect.''

''Do not be intoxicated by tasting this honey. You have to do a lot in the world further. Let us first clean the balcony and then go to the river bank to have a walk.''

''I took-up a broom. I understood that my guru was teaching me the lesson of balanced life. While keeping busy in the thought of the world and its creation, one should also do his routine duty.''

The Guru, makes the disciple aware of the world consciousness. The disciple makes his mind so firm as not to be terrified by looking at the strange sights. Only mental resolutions are not sufficient. The inner urge of self-realisation, the inner call and the prayer are necessary equipments of Sadhana.

It is the firm rule of nature that the Sadhak is blessed with divine experiences. His strong desire to unite with God, leads him fast towards God. God also, looking at the love and submission of the Sadhak, and charmed by his devotion, appears before him.

Yoganand has described his Samadhi experiences as follows:-

The experiences of Samadhi are unexpected beyond imagination and blissful Samadhi state is not a state of unconsciousness. On the contrary it is present in full conscious form."

In one of his Bengali poems, he sings:-

"The veils of light and shade have shattered. The feelings of grief have gone for him, the sense of past, present and future has vanished."

"My 'I' has become universal. I am feeling eternal peace and happiness.

"After my first experience of Samadhi state, I remained in that state for months. I realised the truth of the statement of the Upanishads," रसो वै स: He is RASA."

About Anahad Nad (sound), Swami says," This (Anahad Nad) is the hum of the speeding instrument of creation, and a proof of the existence of God. The new Sadhak listens to this sound and comes to believe about his contacts with the higher spheres. Anahad Nad is surc means of God realisation.

LIGHT: Christ has said:

"The word was in the beginning; it was with God, and was God Himself. Everything came out of that. Whatever was created, was not without Him. He had life and life became the light of man."

Swamiji says: "The vedic (ॐ) became the Hum of the (हूँ) Tibetians, Amin (अमीन) of the Muslims, Greeks, and Jews and Omen (ओमन) of the Christians. About Samadhi Swamiji says:-

"The state of Savikalpa Samadhi is the initial stage of God union. In this state the consciousness of the Sadhak, associates with the cosmic consciousness. His pranic energy is ejected out human body. Externally the body becomes motionless but internally remains active. When it reaches the nirvikalpa state after long efforts, he can keep his consciousness alive even while discharging his worldly responsibilities."

Yukteshwarji also says:

"The ancient yogis had discovered that the breath has a poignant relationship with God realisation. This is the main contribution of Bharat to the world knowledge. The pranic energy, that is usually consumed in regulating the breathing process is to be kept in reserve for higher purposes. Therefore the saints and the yogis have advised to Jap Mantra, with the breathing. In Budh religion Vipashyana (विपश्यती) is fully based on the process of breathing."

Regarding the miracles during Sadhana

As the physical rules regard the physical miracles as the result of scientific process similarly the rules of nature operate behind the spiritual miracles. When the Sadhak becomes aware of them, they become simple happennings to him. No miracle physical, material or spiritual, is out of the rules of nature. It remains a miracle only untill we come to know about the rules."

"Physical science is unable to reach God. It can just find out the rules and the principles. It is quite incapable of finding out God."

"When the Sidhas raise themselves from the ordinary consciousness and achieve the aim of union with God, they unveil, the secret of creation. So long as man is under the illusion of dwait, (dualify) he can not realise God.

"Most modern discoveries are based on the magnetic qualities of light. The Sidha Yogi makes miracles with the help of these light rays. As the movement of the fine pictures appears real on account of the combination of light and reflection, similarly the appearances of the worldly objects are mere illusions. God provides recreation and amusement to His children through this activity i.e. making the people play different roles in the universal stage. He adds:

"When, in an informative film I saw a horrid seen of human massacre, I left the cinema hall. I prayed and asked God as to why this takes place. The reply was that the scene that are being enacted in France, are the films of the play, being staged elsewhere also in the world. They are false and illusive like the pictures of the film."

The divine voice said further.

"The creation is both light and shadow. Else the making of any film, would not be a possibility. My children are the children of light. They shall not remain in delusion for ever. The creation is like a vast film and its reality lies not with the creation but beyond that."

Describing one of such experiences, he says:

I was sitting in Padmasan (पदमासन). I saw that small particles of light, like the mustard seeds of various colours, are twinkling under the roof. They rained upon me, like the drops of rain. Immediately my physical existence melted away into Subtle one. I felt as if I were floating. I moved upon the weight less bed towards right and left. The walls and the furniture were firm as before. But the numbers of light practicals increased to the extent that I could not see the roof. I was wonder struck rather."

"I saw my arms and turned them but I did not feel any weight. For a long time, I continued to watch the film of my body in the scant lighted theatre of my bedroom. The illusion of my concrete body gave way completely and my understanding that the reality of all objects is light only, became fully firm."

Swami Muktanand

In the present era, Swami Muktananad, the founder of 'SIDHA PITH', Ganeshpuri (Bombay) occupies a prominent place among the saints who have revealed the secrets of the experiences of awakening of the Kundalini. He was born in 1908, in a wealthy family of South Karnatak. He left his home at the age of fifteen in search of his Guru.

In 1947 he met Swami Nityanand ji and he received his Prasad, in the form of Saktipat Diksha (शक्तिपात दीक्षा). He penanced for a long time in some lonely place. In 1956 he spent sometime with his Guru Nityananad ji. He became the Adhisthata (अधिष्ठाता) of the Ashram after guru's death. He made a foreign tour in 1970. He provided Shaktipat Diksha to thousands of the native and foreign people. The ashram flourished well, under his super vision and control. He became famous in the spiritual world.

He took his Mahasamadhi in 1982.

The only purpose of Swamiji's life was to bring out the God element, concealed in man. He opined that the grace of the Guru and Shaktipat were the best means of realisation. He has given a detailed account of his experiences in his book "Chitshakti Villas", (चित शक्ति विलास)'

Swamiji even before his passing away, had declared Swami Chidvilasanand and his brother Swami Nitya Nand, as his descendent disciple, who proved very worthy followers.

Swami Muktanand State:

"As in the physical science so in the spiritual field, a vast store of mysterious knowledge is hidden. According to Sidhyog, man is the master of immense divine powers known as Kundalini power. But we don't know it. It's knowledge comes to the Sadhak through his Guru. This power in an advanced stage, leads to God realization. The Jeev begins to feel himself, Sachchidanand Swarup."

"The Sadhana that seems very tough to practise, becomes very easy with the help of Shaktipat. The Sadhana becomes deeper and deeper, leading the Sadhak to its consumation. He feels himself fully fulfilled with god realisation.

Swamiji, himself had reached the realised state by following the same process. He in his turn, obliged innumberable Sadhaks' with this method. He declared the realisation the result of the Grace of God only.

He writes:

"I have stated again and again that the Chit Shakti (Kundalini), the power of God, operates in many ways. It makes the Sadhak do many yogic exercises with its grand, joyous and blissful inspirations. These exercises cause great wonder to the Sadhak. He makes strange expressions at the movement of this power. The new aspirant dances, sings, moves and turns, shouts and cris hopes like a frog and performs asanas and mudras of different kinds. Trembling, and perspiring take place. Mool Bandh, Jalandhar Bandh and Uddiyan bandh happen automatically. Sometimes, the tongue sticks to the Palate, in the Kheechari Mudra. The pupils of the eyes stketch upwards and staring at some object begin by themselves. All these changes do take place according to the state of the Sadhak. Different pranayam's like Bhasrika, Ujjain, Keval etc. happen by themselves. As the practice advances external reactions diminish, giving place to the internal one's . If, there is some suppressed disease, it also goes out. The Sadhak sometimes appears like an intoxicated person. He witnesses various scene and sights before his eyes. The Anahad Nad and lights of different colours also become audible and visible.

"The Sidhas, gods, heavens, hells and Sidha lokes etc. come to sight. The Sadhak wanders into space. Waves of divine joy start flowing in the veins. The Sadhak seems living in a happy place full of love for all and pity too."

"The force of power fluctuates now and then. Advising the Sadhaks, he says.

"Ye, Sadhaks! Be not afraid. Rely on the Guru fearlessly. Meditate regularly. Observe Yamas and Niyamas. Repeat the Guru Mantra.

The experiences and the appearances which Swami Muktanand has described differ according to the states of the Sadhaks. He advises not to be engrosed in them. One should proceed on and on at the instance of the inner voice. In the beginning, physical interactions take place but later on, the subtle things happen. Sometimes the interactions, cease completely. Describing his personal experiences, he says:

"I kept my eyes closing and opening. A flood of light blazened inside. Very tiny sparks shone beautifully. I opened the eyes to see outside. Very strange and beautiful scenes were revealed during meditation.

He felt that the Kundalini power was causing purity in him. It was uprooting the deep delved Sanskaras completely.

With the purity of the Nadis, Pran and the senses, the duration of meditation also increased. New experiences started taking place. He got an insight through which he could see the whole world. Now, his attention was centred on the subtle from the material. In place of red, he saw white light now, the mysterious light. After sometime his meditation was transferred to the blue flame in the causal body. Later on all the flames appeared intermingled into one another. Then the illumined blue star only remained. He travelled other spheres on the blue vehicle. He felt different kinds of smells also during the Dhyan and heard divine sweet songs and sounds. An unique fearlessness came to him. The river of love started flowing. After having realised God, he felt fulfilled, fully content and peaceful. About Guru he says:

"The Guru energies the internal powers and enables him to enjoy the divine happiness. He teaches the disciple yoga, gives him the treasure of knowledge, provides with faith and love, and teaches disconcern or detachment. He gives him liberation. He is not but Shiva."

"The guru should be capable of giving the power of mantra sidhi, and causing Shaktipat. He should be able to transfer his powers. There is no sex distinction in Guru, Shiva is guru and Parashakti is also guru, with the blessings of the guru and the awakening of the Yog mother Kundalini, all the carnal evils subside and the discrimation of man and woman vanishes. After the awakening of the Kundalini the fleshy body remains but the mind becomes pure and conscious. Under such state only the Chitshakti of God works, without any distinction of male or female feelings." He says that his guru was one of such Sidhas. Divine consciousness flowed from him in the form of light rays. Whoever, looked at him, was soon awakened.

At the time of initiation, the power of guru goes into the Shishya. As there is tree, in the seed, similarly the Guru-Chetna also unfolds the yogi in the Shishya and makes him perform various Kriyas of yog. These Kriyas are neither meaningless nor fruitless. The Paramguru interacts there various Asanas, Pranayams, Dances, Mantra Jap and Mudras etc. are got done by the Guru Shakti. The on-lookers, may find them strange. and fearful but the Sadhak is never terrified. He feels elated. Really when the disciple enters the energy sphere of the guru, every exercise is performed easily.

The Sadhan starts with the blessing of the Sidhas, some start experiences sooner and some later. If the Sadhana is internal, it is not known. Even if there is no response, the Sadhana should be continued honestly, faithfully, with love and rituals. The blessings of the guru do not go waste.

The Sushumna nerve is the centre of Mahashakti. The awakened Kundalini controls 72000 nerves with the help of Panch Pran. The Kundalini power makes the body firm, pure and attractive by entering into the red blood cells and the Sapta Dhatus.

The Namjap is a great help in the awakening of the power. The Jap should be performed with the chanting of the Mantra given by the guru. The guru lives in the Mantra therefore, the guru mantra should be chanted. It should be chanted by uniting 'Pran' with Apan Vayu. The appearance will take place soon. The guru shakti causes some appearance like light, point or sound for the medium of meditation. It shall go deeper and deeper.

Meditation is the sole means of settling the mind. It is like the Kalpa Vriksha (कल्पावृक्ष) Meditation is the magnet for attracting Godpower. It is not an ordinary means. Dhyan means the mind being thoughtless, peaceful and still. (निर्विषयं मत:). The yogis of higher order only knows about the secret of meditation. Realization through meditation, indicates a very high State. Doubts should not be allowed to persist regarding meditation i.e.. Whether the meditation should be made on Sakar or Nirakar. Both take to the same goal. Be Sans Chitta and one with the soul. This is the process of meditation.

Parashakti

"Parashakti Sri. Kundalini Mahavidya is called Sidha Vidya. The practicenor of this Path is called Sidha-vidyarti. Anyone advancing on the path of Sadhana becomes honourable."

"Be absorbed in the various experiences and remember them with love. Spoil not your pious Vrittis with evil feelings and doings. The following Shloka, brings out the efficacy of Dhyan:

यत्रास्ति मोक्षो न च तत्र भोगो, यत्रास्ति भोगो, न चतत्र मोक्ष

"Where there is Bhog, there can not be Moksha"

श्री सुंदरी सेवन तत्परायणं भोगाश्च मोक्षश्च्च करस्थावेव"

"But where Sri Sundari (Kundalini Shakti) is worshipped, Bhog and Moksha, both live there without any doubt."

When the Kundalini awakens, many yogic interactions happen.

Swami Muktanand describes:

"I sat on the Asana and went into Padmasan posture. A flame of fire, seemed ablaze all around. The whole space seemed to be caught by fire. The ocean burst out, the earth submerged into it. The spirits like ghosts and pishachas surrounded me. In the meantime, my Padmasana changed into Budha Padmasan (बुद्धपदमासन). My eyes closed. My throat suffocated and an acute pain developed in the lower portion of the back on account of sore of the nerve joint, Muladhar. I wanted to run away but my feet were tied into Padmasan. I wanted to close my eyes, but they opened themselves. I saw that a white ball entered my body and my head prostrated on the ground.''

''Sometimes I bleated like a camel and sometime roared like a tiger. I was roaring so loudly that the people thought that a tiger had come into the cane field. This interaction continued for sometime forcefully, but subsided after sometime.''

''As I sat for meditation, a strong red light appeared before me, as if it were residing within me. The two full long blaze of light caused an illumination, I saw clearly that I was burning but without feeling of any burning pain. The murmur of burning fire was audible everywhere. I was absorbed completely into the thought of that light. After some time I felt very hot inside, at the idea of that blazing light.

The Practioners of this system, have experiences of thousand kinds. They are not available for hearing. Even if they are available they are mysterious. No Sadhak or Sidha is there to explain them. Therefore the Sadhak feels afraid and gives up his Sadhana. Due to his ignorance he discourages other aspirants also. That is not good. He should not say that the mind will go mad etc.

As a proof in support of these experiences Saint Gyaneshwar Maharaja says:

The body is like a lotus from nail to top. It has four petals of four types, measures and colours. Every Petail has its own characteristic. The first petal is this physical visible body. It is of red colour. The second is astral one, with the state of sleep and dream. It is eight 'angul' in size. Its colour is white.

The third petal is causal body, equal to the little finger in size and black in colour. The fourth is the Mahakaran body (महाकरण शरीर) which is of the size of a linseed and blue in colour. This fourth body state is of great importance, very radiant and brilliant. It is the root of Sadhana, an entity of the highest innerself.''

''At the awakening of the power (Kundalini) many interactions happen which are purposeful. These interactions (Kriyas) eradicate the diseases and purify the nerves. They are quite different from the physical ones. Ordinarily these Kriyas go on for a longtime. Concentrating on the red light, different experiences take place daily. The power of concentration increases with this red light. The nerves also get purified.''

''So far I did not know that I have been bestowed with the divine Shaktipat. I kept noticing various lights alongwith the red-one. My memory kept working during meditation. I felt gay. While watching the lights, I saw naked man or boy, a cow or the flocks of white horses, temples of my surrounding areas and their idols. I meditated for two hours or more in the morning and in the evening.''

''Often I sprawled like a serpent and hissed likewise. I noticed Cobras many times. The Nag (Cobra) is a manifested form of Mahayogeshwar Shiva. The day of seeing Nag, proved pleasant to me.''

''I twisted my neck forcefully; bending down, and down, my chin touched the 'Kanthkup' (कंठकूप). This posture became the JALANDHAR BANDH OF Hath Yog. With the Jalandhar bandh on, a strange interaction started in the arms and without any effort from myside stopped itself.''

''During the meditation I could see the whole set of Nadis working in the body. The Pran, moving through them also could be seen. Sometime, sitting in the Padmasana, my head touched the ground. All these interactions happened effortlessly. In this way the knowledge of Yog came through intuition. Sometimes the head titled backwards completely and sometimes the eyes were fixed on the nose. During such state the breath came like the furnace of the blacksmith. Sometimes the Pran, went out of the body completely. I came to know latter that it was a kind of Bhasrika Pranayam that eradicated the diseases of the stomach and purified it.

''Formerly I did not know anything about the reactions caused by the awakening of the Kundalini power. Now, it came to be understood by me with the help of some suitable books. My Sadhana galloped fast like the flood of some great river. Everyday, new experiences occurred I meditated after getting up at 3 in the morning (ब्रहममुहूर्त). Just at sitting in meditation, I felt a force, overcoming me. This force made Rakteshwari (the Red light) illumine. The Rakteshwari revealed an oval white ball. It appeared and disappeared again and again. The Rakteshwari remained complete. The three bandhas transfixed by themselves. The heel of the foot, touched the Gudamul (गुदामूल) and the arms squeezed. It was mool bandh. This balances the Pran and the Apan Vayu, keeps away old age and diseases. The Sadhak can acquire the power of keeping himself in the Sunya (शून्य) sitting in the padmasana posture and controlling the Pran. This mudra causes Darduri gati or Mandook Kriya. (दार्दुरी व मंडूक क्रिया है)।

''Side by side of these reactions, the Pran Vayu, exhaled out of the stomach and it pitched inward, making a small pit. It seemed at that time as if the lower air were thrust upward. This is called Uddiyan Bandh, a very important one. After this, the Chin sticks to the throat well, making it into Jalandar Bandh. The drops of nectar that trickle down in the Sahasrar, are burnt up by the sun and fire present in the Nabhi Chakra. With the exercise of this Chakra, the outlet of the nectar flowing down stops and it is saved from being burnt. The mind of the yogi goes very still through this bandh. These three bandhas, i.e. Mool, Uddiyan and Jalandhar give unique result to the user.''

''By and by the Pran and apan united and became balanced. My Padmasan also became Sidh. This perfection or Sidhi is achieved by sitting for three hours continuously. After thri bandh, I used to practise this Mandook Kriya i.e. froglike hopping in my cottage. Every interaction gave great joy. During meditation various Kriyas like Mahamudra, Mahabandh, Biprit Karni, Bajroli etc. took place. Sometimes the bottom of the anus was pressed with the right or left heel. Sometimes I placed my head on the thighs of the stretched legs, holding the toe, with fingers.

This exercise caused the Kundalin to aspir and enter the Sushmna with Pran. All the nerves became active with this, their inertness fully gone!

''Sometimes I placed my feet on each other and sat there. The body then, was filled with air (breath) Jalandhar bandh set on. The breath went out slowly. This posture is called Mahabandh Rudra with this practice, the Pran, enters Sushmna making body and the diaphragm stronger. Sometimes Uddiyan bandh occured during Mahabedh Bandh. The whole Pran abstained outside and the external Kumbak took place. Through this kumbhak the three Brahma, Vishnu and Rudra knots are loosened. The Kundalini reaches the Sahasrar. This type of Sidhi is useful for Pranic control and renewing old age. Sometimes I placed my hands on the earth and placing my head on them stretched my legs upwards for some time. This posture is known as Viparit Karni Mudra or Shirshasan. This asan increases appetite, removing the wrinkles and white hair of the body. This posture stops the flow of nectar downwards, from the Shaharar. In this position, the balance was placed on my two hands the head hung in between. This posture is known as Bajrouli Rudra. It causes success of Bindu, the source of immense power.

''These experiences were followed by Pranayams of different kinds. Some of which are being described here. Sometimes I inhaled air like a serpentess and sometimes, the tongue stuck to the palate, causing Kumbhak to take place. This mudra cures diseases. The tongue becomes capable of entering the Kapal Guha preceding Khechari Mudra. Sometimes I inhaled air, turning my tongue like the beak of a crow. This was called Kaka or Sheetalarudra, the provider of long-life sometimes the Kapa, trickled fearfully and the eyes became transfixed in Moolbandh, making it Shambhavi Mudra. This mudra makes the mind still and peaceful.''

"I witnessed the interactions of the Kundalini again and again. I meditated two or three times daily from three early in the night at noon at eleven and at seven (from seven to Nine) in the evening, often I crawled like a serpent in a zigzag way, hopped like a frog, or roared like a lion. I was rather, spell bound with the appearance of this grace of Bhagwati.

Some Yogi told Muktanand that a Sadhak treading the path of Sidhamarg should regard everything as the form of CHITI - high, low, good, bad, welcome seen, unseen etc. Nothing can exist without Chiti. All the forms and actions in Yogmarg are completly Chiti.

"My Padmasana, became so firm that I could sit for three hours at a stretch. Many interactions started with the tongue. It hung out upto the heart and then, settled back as before I saw visions as if in semi conscious state. I developed faith in the Sadhana, in the guru and in the submission before the Chiti." The body developed such a great heat that even sitting in the cold water tank, could not cool it down."

"One day I saw a large city during meditation and I felt drowsy. While in the state of subconsciousness, I saw a chariot coming."

"I had a new experience then. During the meditation, and at the appearance of the light, I saw myself sitting before me. This continued to appear so, even after opening the eyes. The memory of gurudeva came first then and I went to Ganeshpuri. During the meditation either I saw myself or my Gurudev. My presence with Gurudeva, developed. After reading the books, I came to know that the appearances came like symbols."

"As soon as I sat in meditation, I felt a kind of quiet. Lights of different kinds like red, white, black and blue appeared and caused numbness. I travelled far and wide during half asleep state, seeing everything. By and by, the body became light, slim, agile, disease free and strong. The Madhyanadi, Shushman could be seem operating, its colour being a mixture of Gold and Silver. All the nadis get inspiration from there. Sometimes the Sadhak develops a pain in his back during meditation. This is due to the entering of Kundalini power into veins. Sometimes, there was a new experience. During the occurance of that experience, I saw a mass of oval, hallo of light equal to the size of the little finger. Swateshwar Upashinad describes:

(अगुष्ठ मात्रः पुरुषो अंतरात्मा, सदाज जनानां हृदये समिविष्ठः)

"The Jeewatma, measuring the thumb length resides in every human heart."

"After sometime I saw a light, quite different from the red, black or blue within it, there appeared various lokas. The colour of this light was light saffron. It contained numberless sparks of blue colour in it. It also contained a dim light of golden colour, which was very sweet and charming. In this light, I saw many spectales of wonderful quality. I could reach the Chanderlok easily, so I could reach this lighted place also, I may call it heaven now."

"The sages that avail the pleasures of this lok, are omniscient. The ancient sages of our land, acquired this place, with the meditation power. They could enjoy themselves this place, even in the waking state. I could reach this state only by the grace of God and that too, in meditation. I could see many distant spheres clearly."

"Once I asked guruji, about the sound (नाद). He explained that it was a sound resounding in the inner space, a divine song. This sound is the giver of divine bliss, inspiring the Pashyantee wak (पश्यंती वाग्) and the Chitta. This sound helps the Yogis and the wise, about their own source. Gyaneshwar Maharaj has stated.

"Beyond this sound, lies the Turya house."

Travelling the Sidhalok

"The blue star stood fixed before me, without any movement. I went in and in, the space of Shahasrar and many spheres. Though it seemed very small, I entered it easily. I landed at a place somewhere. The place was very pleasant. I saw a path, many woods, small caves, flowing streams multicoloured deers and white pecocks. The atmosphere was very calm. The space was filled with bluish light seen through a prism, at the time of the rising sun. There was neither the sun nor the moon but there was light enough by itself. I wandered there wilfully. I came to understand that it was Siddha-Lok. I saw numberless Sidhas meditating there, and sitting in different postures. Some had a hood of hair and the others were clean-shaven headded. There were great saints there, like the Sai Baba of Shirdi. Baba Nityanand, though living in Ganeshpuri, was there of course.

"The light there was very brilliant. I saw many Yoginis there. I wandered there for long. Then, I saw a pond, full of lotuses. I could not ascertain the kind of trees there. I wished to sit in Padmasana and meditate. But the blue star appeared and I took my seat in it. It carried me speedily to the spot of meditation. I entered the state of semi-consciousness. A Sidha, from Sidha Lok appeared there and said, "The place that you visited just, was Sidhalok The people liberated from life and birth, live there. After that I descended below, reciting Onkar (ओंकार), I bowed to my guru. I opened my eyes but found nothing." Saint Tuka Ram, who had realised God, says:-

"The seekers of the path of realisation see God, face to face. God lives in a small house built of the size of a Til (Linseed). He is called the sustainer because he sustains the whole creation. He lives in a tiny home like the huge tree that lives in a small seed. The unity of God is kept in whole in the tiniest thing. He is whole and beyond all effects. The three worlds live within him, the heaven, the hell, the subterranean (पाताल) are the (भूर्भुवःस्वः) all contained in Him.

"The Jeevatma, has four sheaths of body. They have been described as knowledge, white black and blue. The red is the physical body and the white, the astral, the black the causal and the blue, the supercausal (महाकारण) body. The super causal is in the centre of the Nileshwari, equalling the size of a linseed. You can understand that in meditation only. Not only this, Hari (विष्णु), Har (Shiv) and Brahma (प्रजापति) all the three come out of this point. This point is the shelter of images and idols. The person who has witnessed this blue point, is indeed a very pious person 'SKANDA PURANA' describes.

कुलं पवित्रं जननी कृतार्थ वसुंधरा पुण्यवती च तेन।
अपार संवित सुख सागरे अस्मिन, लीन परे बह्मणि यस्य चेतः

"He Who realises God is supposed to lie in an ocean of bliss. His Kul becomes pious, mother becomes fulfilled and not only that; the whole world becomes virtuous."

Shri Jitendra Bhartiya

Shaktipat :

The mountain Dronagiri lies in the north of Dwarahat City in Almora district. At the top of this mountain, there is a temple of Vaishnau Devi. In 1962, Shri Jitendra Chandra Bhartiya and Pt. Vidya Sagar Joshi of Lucknow, reached there to participate in the Shatchandi Yagna, held there. There they met Shri Swami Onkaranand Tirth. After some formal talk Shri Swamiji asked them to go to his cottage taking a blanket only. Led by the eagerness of knowing Shri Vidya Sagar did not wait for the morning even and reached the cottage of Swamiji the same night. The Swami was in meditation and a lamp was lit. Joshiji spread his blanket and sat silently. When Swami ji opened his eyes he said that Joshi was asked to come in the morning. Joshi replied that he had gone and would go away again the next morning also. If Swamiji pleased, he could tell him about some Sadhana. Swamiji asked him to go and to wait for tomorrow. Joshiji continued to sit even then Swamiji was not annoyed. He tried to console him like a mother, Who consoles an obstinate child. He asked Joshi to sit in any posture he liked. He sat and closed his eyes. He pronounced the high sound of (ॐ) Omkar. As soon as he heared this sound, he forgot his presence and became silent, dumb, feelingless, senseless. Such was the wonder of his pronunciation. He did not remember how long he remained in that state. When he came to his senses, the Swami said that his work was done. He asked him (Joshi) to sit like that every day. He took his leave and returned to his abode. He was under a great intoxication, he went to bed quietly.

The next day, he reached the cottage of Swamiji again, alongwith Bhartiya Ji. Swamiji ordered them to sit apart. He started his sidhpranayam, pronouncing the Onkar Dhawni, that shook the earth and the sky. The body of Bhartiya also started trembling. Different kinds of yog kriyas, Assans and mudras, pranayam etc. started taking place automatically. Strangely enough, there was no reaction of anykind in Joshi. He simply, kept sitting and watching the interactions in Bhartiyaji. He did not close his eyes, fearing that he may not go into oblivion himself and may be deprived of seeing the wonderful interactions in Bhartiyaji. It all finished within an hour and Swamiji asked them to go after blessing them. Swamiji also said that it was a kind of Shaktipat. Mahamaya Jagdamba was pleased with them and their Kundalini power had awakened. Thus, both of them had their initiation done. After this they sat before the guru two times more on next days. On the third day they left. Jitendraji had tears in his eye. His condition was like the daughter's departure from the house of her father. Gurudeva blessed him and said that his speech shall be an expression of Goddess Saraswati.

The Divine Declaration

As a result of the blessing given by Guruji, after five months of the occurance, divine oracle started coming out through the speech of Bhartiyaji. At the time of his speaking the tape recorder was set on. This recording was done every evening and morning during meditation.

In the begining, Mother Saraswati pronounced Sanskrit Sutras (सूत्र) regarding the Shaktipat Vidya. Later, she explaimed these in Sanskrit. After sometime, the spirit of Yogiraj Gorakhnath appeared in Bhartiya and both Yogiraj and Saraswati spoke through Bhartiya. When, Bhagwati Saraswati spoke in Sanskrit, it was translated into the vernacular by Gorakhnath. Mother Saraswati said herself that these Vidyas had been lost and though it was all secret it was being explained for the good of the people.

After Shaktipat :

The Shaktipat Mahayagn is a very airy and tedious path. Samarth Guru Ramdas, could infuse power in his disciple through Shaktipat and energize his Kundalini with the grace of the Goddess. Afterward, the awakened power, makes the disciple do different Asanas, Pranayames, Mudras, Kriyas etc. by themselves. The blessing of the Guru, is the chief cause in the Shaktipat Sadhana. In other systems, the Asanas etc. are attempted to arouse the Kundalini Shakti. There is some times success and sometimes a failure. But in the Shaktipat Sadhana, the Kundalini awakens first and then interactions follow. The disciple may know or may not know these things but they do happen. This is the difference between Shaktipat and other Sadhanas. This path is divine.

The Ancient Yog :

If aum and Ram are treated as the common name for God, there remains no difference between our aims and realizations. You shall see no difference in the systems of Swami Ramanand Ji and Omkarnath. The experience, that have been described and all of them have been possible by the grace of the Swami Mahashakti Saraswati. Our Gurudev has called that path as the path of Ascent.

The Shastra that has been given expression by Shri Bhartiya, has been named, "Sarswati Kundalini Mahayog." (कुण्डलिनी महयोग). I wish to bring to the light of the Sadhaks, these experiences only that are semilar to those of ours.

In the begining of the Shaktipat Avtaran, Maa Saraswati explains about the special experience:

One should develop an urge for the Sakhtipat. Faith, Belief and Resolve are inevitable for understanding the secret of Shaktipat. The difficulties that come in the way must also be understood properly.

The urge develops only when the Mahashakti wishes otherwise not ''The wish of Mahashakti occurs only with the help of the Guru because Guru himself meets with the blessings of God. If wit and wisdom prevail favourably, the power to understand interactions arises. The able Gurus always test the disciple before initiating him.

When the capacity of experiencing and realizing develops, the inspirations come. The knower of Kundalini Vigyan, know well about that. They are generally in the form of the visions of present, future of Sidhas, and Goddesses etc. Talks with them and receiving inspirations etc. also take place.

The Shaktipat helps in the inner realizations. As the sprouting takes place in the seed, similarly fresh realizations also come to the Sadhak. The realizations occur either through the grace of the super mother or through the Shaktipat done by the Guru. When the self-power and the Supreme Power Unites, Mahashakti arises in the Sadhak. The experiences and appearances take place in a casual or an ordered sequence. The 'Vrittis' calm down by themselves. This is the Integral or Antar (आन्तर) Yog. (योगः चित्तवृतिनिरोधः)

When the senses are attatched with the objects the mind is more fickle. Sensuality increases due to this. But the Param Shakti itself works, the state of Nirodh is created; the fickleness vanishes and the state of Dhyan develops. All the desires pass away. In the absence of Bhog, the diseases also disappear. The senses are controlled by the Supreme Power and the 'vrittis' subside. Through Meditation Param or Pratyabhas (प्रत्यामास) take place.

In this way, meditation develops the experienced knowledge and the knowledge helps in bringing about meditation state. Therefore it has been stated that the one knowing 'Dhyan' and 'Gyan', becomes successful in crossing over the ocean of the World. Knowledge does not come without

'Dhyan' and one who is not Yogi, can not meditate. 'Dhyan' is subordinated to Pranayam and this Pranayam is taught by Mahashakti Kundalini. That Pranayam would be a Sidha one and is the result of the grace of Mahashakti. Therefore the Mother, first regulates the senses and then controls the mind. Shakti is possible through grace and so Shaktipat is the only way of gathering Shakti.

The Path of DESCENT (अवरोह) is a bit different. In this Path, everything comes through grace. Whatever, the Sadhak needs is given by the Mother. Mind is subordinate to Pran, which is fickle by nature. The anyam of Pran makes the mind firm and still.

Then comes the state of awareness (बोधावस्था). In this state also, there is only meditation. The realization of PARAM comes by itself. The light in the heart increases, causing delight more and more. In that state the mind does not like to go anywhere". I am the one (सोऽह्मस्मि) 'Vritti' fixes the mind to that idea. Then the knowledge of the self comes and knowledge flows out like a stream.

The awareness or state of real knowledge is brought about by the Mahashakti itself. It provides both Shiva and Shakti. Real knowledge (तत्वज्ञान) is never possible without the transmission of power (शक्तिपात) and as such every Sadhak should aspire and yearn for that. Shaktipat leads naturally to reality and praticality. Only the grace of the Guru can provide Shakti.

Bodhavastha (State of realization) is followed by Sidhavastha. In that state the Supreme Kundalini Mahamaya makes the Sadhak realise the state of Jagriti (जागृति). It is said about Sidhavastha: "The Sidhavastha is that in which Sadhaks visualise the parampad and which is the state of bliss, it is the state in which the mahayogi, Sidhas realise Soham (सोऽह्म) state, a state which is true, blissful, eternal, Nirvikalpa and Nirashaya leading to the realization of God. No doubt is left after that.

हेयाः सिद्धयः (The Sidhis are denouncible)

Undoubtly, Sidhis come to the Sadhaks to present their forms but they prove a cause of hinderance in the Sadhana. Therefore, the Sidhis are denounced by sages and Sadhaks. If only one Sadhak wishes to use those Sidhis in the good of humanity, they should be used only after seeking permission of the Guru. However, the Sidhis should be regarded as hurdles (विक्षेप). Only a complete Yogi can put them to profit. Only rare Yogis dare give up the prosperity acquired through the perfection in their Sadhana, for proceeding further on the path. It is only with the strength of God, that the Mumukshus (मुमुक्षु) advances on the path of realization, giving up the charms and attractions of the Sidhis in use.

The Symptoms of Shaktipat

When a deserving conditioning (सानुकूलता) happens in the Sadhak, the Guru provides him with Shaktipat. He energises the sleeping Kundalini of the Sadhak with his own power. The power of the Guru Strengthens the powers of the Sadhak. After the practice of Kriyayog, different asanas, mudras and interactions happen because the Shakti struggles to soar up for Yog Sidhi. It is said:

सम्प्राप्ते चं क्रिया योगे, नाम्ना कार्यवती सती।
सा शक्ति जृम्भतेचोर्ध्व तस्माद योगः प्रसिद्धियति।।

The Shaktipat can be discerned through symptoms in the form of heat in the body. Trembling, prespiration and tearshedding. These are the prelimenary symptoms of Shaktipat. In the second state the breathing becomes broken, the Shaking of the limbs of the body takes place. Sounds like the barking of the dogs, the howling of the jackals and the roaring of the lions are also uttered.

The third symptom of an energised person is that he begins to feel ecstasy and growth of knowledge inside. These symptoms are good and according to the State of the aspirant. It is said:

लक्षणानि च प्राक्तानि भंसरधानि वराणीच।
समये समये शक्तिः स्वयमेव प्रणशयेत।।

The symptoms are numerous and the Shakti reveals them occasionally. These symptoms should satisfy the Sadhak about his Kundalini Shaktijagaran.

The Shakti Jagaran is possible with the grace of Guru or God only. But the question is how to get the grace?

The grace shall fail if the pure sanskaras do not live in the Sadhak. So, the Sadhak should prepare himself accordingly.

The grace or favour rains upon the Sadhak according to his deservings. The sameness or thoughts etc. is equally found in the Guru and the disciple for getting the grace, some kriyas are also necessary. For example though wood, stone and iron, lie side by side, the magnet reacts on iron only. So, the Guru also helps the deserving disciple in times of difficulty. If there is affinity between the Guru and the Shishya, the Shaktipat will be possible soon.

The Shaktipat is of three kinds: through the vision, through touch and through sparsh. The Guru with his own kundalini awakened, energises that of the disciple. He flows his shakti dormant at his nave, through his eyes. The Kundalini of the Shishya also becomes energised. The aspiring current of power of the Guru, enters the body of the Shishya. The Scriptures explain the meaning of Gu (गु) as darkness and of Ru (रु) as eradication.

अज्ञानतिमिरान्धस्य, ञानांजन शलाकया।
चक्षुरुन्मीलितं येन, तस्मै श्री गुरु वे नमः।।

The small rod, using ointment of the eye, removes the ignorance (blindness) like the grace of the Guru. That Guru has to be revered and respected.

The mysterious power remains hidden within the body of every being but the one who brings it forth, is called the competent Guru.

The Shaktipat is possible through touch also. The spot between the two eyebrows is called Triputi. This is the spot of Mahabodh and mantra as well. The perfect or competent Sadguru touches it. The mere touch materlises the Shakti at Muladhar, going through the Sushumna Marg. The Guru touches the Triputi with the thumb and the Shakti is aroused soon. The Shakti entering through the Triputi goes through Sushuman marg to Mulagdhar and energises the dormant Kundalini there with the union of the Guru Shakti, it awakens and reacts for soaring up. This state should be regarded as the state of Shaktipat.

शम्भो मा शाम्भवी शक्तिः तं प्राप्तं चेष्ठते यदा।
तदा नाना क्रिया सद्यो जापन्ते साधो शुभाः ।।

"When the Shiva-Shakti desires union with Shiva different kinds of interactions start taking place in the Sadhak."

The Guru Shakti passes into the disciple through touch also as:

सुप्ता कुन्डलिनी देवी स्पर्शनादेव जागृत।
तस्मात स्पर्शनिकारेण दीक्षां कुर्यतिक्रिचित बुद्याः।।

"The Kundalini awakens at the touch of the Guru, therefore certain Gurus awaken the power of the Shishya through touch."

The Shaktipat is possible through words also the Mantra is spoken to the Shishya and the Kundalini is energised. The Sadguru utters the mantra and makes the shishya repeat it. This practice is also used by some for Shaktipat.

The Shaktipat is sometime, done through resolve or wish, in cases where the Guru and Shishya are distantly situated. These are all the processes and means of Shaktipat.

Benefit of Shaktipat

Shaktipat is done for the awakening of power which lies sleeping or inactive. The first purpose of Shaktipat is to enable the Sadhak for the exercise of asanas, Pranayams, Purifications of the nervous system and the energising of the Chakras.

शम्भौविमुक्ताया शक्तिः, शाम्भवी दिव्यारूपिणी।
तत्संयोगं परमलक्ष्मं परब्रह्मणीलीनता ।।

The best aim of Shaktipat is to bring about the Union of Shiva and Shiv into Brahma.

Lord Shiva resides in Kailash and Bhagwati Bhawani Shakti lives in Muladhar. So, the purpose of the Shaktipat is to cause the union of both powers. So long as Shiv is apart from his Shakti and does not unite with it perfection can not come. Therefore, the wise should get the union done first. The Sadhak's endeavour therefore, should always be for this mutual union.

The benefits of Shaktipat are great. It provides powers of the physical as well as astral world. Efforts should be made to know and realise Brahma, to see and to dissolve in him. The deh Sidhi (देहसिद्धि) and other sidhis are of immense benefit.

The Sadhak initiated into the path through Shaktipat acquires the state of mahasmadhi and the Rajyog, Hathyou, Layayog, Mantra Yog and others consumate by themselves. The greatest advantage of Shaktipat is the attainment of bliss the happiest feeling of realising the Partatva (परतत्व) and getting dissolved into it.

Shakti acquired through Chakrabhedan

The power of Shaktipat rises up and up to cause an union of Shiva and Shiv. First it cleans the path and removes all the obstacles of reaching the destination. It creates the urge of observing Pranayam and consequently aspiring for Grandhibhedan. It first removes the Mal (Refuge) and clears the path of march.

प्राणाममैर्विना नाणीशोधनं न भवेत क्वाचित।
तदर्थं चेष्ठमेत सद्यः सा देवी परमेश्वरी।।

"Nadi Shadhan is not possible without Pranayam and for that purpose the Shakti itself endeavours".

Those without the knowledge of 'Antarang Yog' (आन्तरयोग) and know only the external one, try to argue every thing through intellect and satisfy themselves with the illusive knowledge got through their imagination. Illusive knowledge prevails where 'Antragyan' is seen in 'Anatma'. But the para Shakti operating itself, there can not by any delusion. It does not allow any ignorance to exist. As the darkness can not exist in light, similarly any kind of ignorance can not exist under Shaktipat. As it is quite wrong to say that there is no sun behind the clouds, similarly, it is wrong to expect or fear any wrong knowledge behind the Shakti. God can only be realised.

Swami Satyanand

Swami Satyanand is one of those grand personalities who have sacrified all their lives for the freedom of their nation, caste and religion. The sacred sound of Ram Nam, was popularised by him echoing throughout the directions. Reverent Ramaand got guru-diksha from this very saint. Therefore he is more respectable for us.

Swamiji took birth in 1861 in a religious Muhyal Brahmin family. His village was called 'Jaggruka Mora' in Rawalpindi district. He was brought up in a village 'ANKARA' at the river Jhelum in Jammu State. He was deprived of paternal affection in his childhood. His grand father and mother (Maternalside) brought him up. The grandfather (NANA) called him Govinda.

The grandmother (NANI) also left him at the age of 10. He started wandering here and there. Fortunately he came into contact with some saints. He developed a desire to study Sanskrit and to lead a purely religious life. He started learning with this view. He was very brilliant and intelligent and he assimilated all that he studied. His teacher was attracted to him for his wisdom and intelligence.

At the age of 16 he had an association of Jain Saints. Inspired by their discourse, he left his house and started living with these Saints. After one year Jain dharma sadhana, he became a Jain Yati and started preaching Jain religion. He made a deep study of Sadhan Granthas and practised also accordingly. Almost all the Shastras pointed out that the Sadhak should have faith in omnipotent, omnipresent and Sachidanand God but the jain philosophy being anti this philosophy an obstruction was caused, in his Sadhana. So, he gave up Jain religion and joined Aryasamaj at the age of thirty.

Whle in Aryasamaj he developed nearness with Mahatma Munshiram (later known as Swami Shardhanand). He started preaching from the Aryasamj platform on mainly the upanishads. He studied Vedanta Sutra and other Vedic literature slowly and slowly.

Those were the days when 'Shastrarthas' were very popular when he entered a war of wit with an opponant, the scene was worth enjoying the audience heard him spellbound and bestowed high praise on him. He wrote many books, the first being "ONKAR UPASANA". Others like

'Dayanand Prakash' was written after great research and study. He had a great quest for spiritual knowledge. He remained in search of the Saints of higher order. In 1925, he chose lonely "DALHOUSI" in the Himalayas for his secluded Sadhana. He determined to sit in meditation at that place till he had complete realization.

After one month of this hard penance on the day of 'Vyas Paurnima' while he sat in meditation, closing his eyes, he heard the word Ram, in a very attractive and charming voice. He opened his eyes but there was none. After closing the eyes again he heard the repeated sound of 'Ram' as before, followed by the instruction "Ram Bhaj", "Ram Bhaj". That word sound was not an ordinary one, the mere sound of the word caused Vibrations in him. He prayed and the word came to him again. He further requested it to appear before him. The voice enquired as to what form he would like to witness. Swamiji said that it might appear in whatever form it is." Then it appeared in the form of 'Ra' and 'M'. That brilliant word light entered his body at once.

At that time, an idea came to his mind about the fact that God manifests himself in Guru form in every age. Therefore, 'Ram' is the Guru Supreme. He is omnipresent. This idea, drove away all other thoughts. Tears of gratefulness trickled from his eyes. He resolved then and there to spend his life in the spreading of this Ram Nam.

He was now infused with the Divine power of Ram. Complete 'Astika Bhawana' took place in him. He started attaining Yogic and Spiritual benefits. He felt that Ram had accpted him and he had become an instrument of Ram.

After becoming fully realised, he started initiating disciples with 'Ram Nam' with effect from 1928 freely.

He wrote many books with a view to creating faith in 'Ram Nam'. Bhakti Prakash is very famous among them. It contains the eulogy of 'Ram Nam'. The managers of Aryasamaj felt displeased at this. They suggested Swamiji, to get the book reprinted by replacing the word Ram with aum. Swamiji refused to oblige them and said that he could leave Aryasamaj and never 'Ram Nam'. He severed connection with Arya Samaj and devoted all of his time in distributing the prasad of 'Ram Mahamantra.'

He wrote "Balmiki Ramayan Sar", in Doha and Chaupai form. 'Amrit Vani', also explains the power of 'Ram Nam' in Doha and Chaupai. In addition he wrote 'Ekadashou panishad' and Shrimad Bhagwat Geeta". He started satsang also for the spiritual uplift of the Sadaks. He advised the Sadaks to practise Sadhana during the four or five days of the week. He wished well for all. He prayed to God for the success of those that were engaged in the well being of the people.

He was a staunch disciplinarian. He could take food with those only with whom he lived. He did not accept any presents. He left for heavenly abode on 13.11.1960 at the age of 99.

The Purpose — Establishment in Ram Nam State

He once said, "You have come here for Sadhana. The aims should be fulfilled at the place where the purpose is 'Ram Nam' Jap only. When the faith is firm, the Ram Ras enters the body and arouses energy also.

NAD (SOUND)

Meditation provides peace and concentration. The Nad (Cosmic sound) is caused by the motions of the spheres. Divine sound also comes occosionally. The Sadhak who regards the 'Nad' as his ultimate hampers his own development. Our purpose is to establish the soul in self, with out this, nothing is useful.

The faithful realize the efficacy of 'Ram Nam' by themselves. The realisations of sincere devotees are far greater than those who undergo difficult penance for long. Such Sadhaks become extra ordinarily ecstatic. The subconscious mind satarts working and the conscious one stops. This is a special state, not an ordinary one. The behaviorial mind stops and the consciousness awakens. The Sadhaks who do not realise the importance of this state, have to regret later.

The saints uplift the persons near them like the mother birds, bringing up their young ones. As the crocodile warms up its eggs through sight only, similarly the saints rain favour on them. The crocodile mothers warms its eggs through sight only. Similarly the Guru inspires the Sadhak with touch, with sight, and with resolve only.

Swatma Prateeti

Feeling of one's own 'self' is called 'Swatma Prateeti.' It is always nice to look high at ones self. The soul should never be looked down upon. This would be an insult to it. Faith and determination reveals the soul. The expression of 'Gyata' and 'Geya', Bhav do not reveal the soul. The soul is felt by the thought that this body is not "mine". I am separate from the body. The hands and feet have become very heavy and the body numb and small. It is very large. It is not necessary that all these experiences should come to every Sadhak. Different kinds of experiences take place in different Sadhaks. If one does not experience anything, but if he acquires concentration, it is a sign of his progress inside.

Further development leads to Ajapa Jap. It means that the Jap is not done with speech, it goes on by itself. The soul has the power to speak, even without senses and the body. Maharishi Patanjali says that the soul creates a 'chitta' through resolve. So, it is not correct to say that we work with intellect or sense. The Atma should bc involved repeatedly by thinking that, "I am Sat, Nitya, Shuddha, Chaitanya, Shakti Man Atma. The affirmation of this idea helps in self realization.

ECSTASY — A kind of SAMADHI

When the rays of the name of Ram, fall on the heart it blooms like anything. When there is no hesitation, there is ecstasy. It acts inside like the electric current. But people have little belief in them. The ecstasy (Masti) is a kind of Samadhi. The person forgets, external things when filled with this joy. There are many people of Godly grace. They watch wonderful things and their body becomes illumined with the atamic lights. The people should have belief in them. 'Ram Nam' is like an electric point house.

The appearance of this 'Dev Bhav' is rewarded further. This is divine state and man acquires sounds impossible for the ordinary people. This is state where a man can have celestial knowledge. He can listen to the distant sounds like an instrument. The radio instruments also capture sounds and the telescopes can discern even moon clearly. A sadhak of this state can do so without any external aid or instruments. This capability comes, slowly. It is not a thing to be laughed at and so they are not stated everywhere.

The Vision of God

The image of God is of different kinds in different people. The 'Vaishnavas' worship God in the foum of Shrikrishna or Vishnu. If the vision of their liking comes, they call it visiting God. It is true also because God manifests through resolve (संकल्प). These Sadhaks who regard God formless, the manifestation for them is difficult because God can not appear in any form.

The Sadhak developes many images in his meditation. He should understand that these images proceed from that kind of resolve, as can be seen in the case of smoke, frost, sun, fire, moon, divine light, air etc. Some sadhaks have the visions of (Avataras) incarnations. This is called, 'Ilham' and 'Adhesh' also. The state of peace, laya, Sunn, etc. is also the same. The consciousness remains there. There is natural affinity between sound and form. Just at the pronouncing a word, a form is created in the astral field and the image of God, appears with that.

The Sadhak feels nearness to God, God is with me, within me. It should never be thought that in the absence of certain symptoms the state is a lonely one. Every Sadhak can not have everything.

The sign of progress - The Signs

(i) Ajapa Jap

"The inspiration of "NAM" or 'Ajapa Jap' is a kind of Yog in which the power appears automatically. Sometime, the name seems to vibrate itself in the mouth, in the heart or in any limb or part of the body. The Sadhak should know then that the recitation goes on naturally inside. This is a very high state. A Sadhak, having reached this state, has no fear of retracing. This state is called 'Sidhavastha', because the aid of the Sadhak becomes the unity of word and nam.

(ii) Concentration (एकाग्रता)

Establishing into self (स्वरूप) is called concentration. It retains consciousness. It is not being completely numb. Samadhi is that state Where the concentration, remaines uninterrupted during working or walking. Samadhi is not that posture only when a Sadhak sits on a seat by closing his eyes.

(iii) NAD (ध्वनि)

The 'NAD' is also one of the symptoms. In the begining it is strong but slowly and slowly it becomes lighter and lighter. This 'Nad' is 'Atmagati' as well as 'Pravitigati'. It is rhythmic also, extremlly sweet. The atma has 'Nad' and even the vibraions caused by the rays of the sun is musical. The charming power of these Nadas, over-whelms the heart.

The 'Atmagati Nad' provides a resonance inside. The 'Nad' is beyond all the Samadhis. Alongwith the 'Nads' there descend words and as such 'Nad' is very mysterious. These are words and natural sounds both. The sound resembles that of the Bee (भ्रमर) or of the echo of the case. It is very sweet and subtle.

LIGHT

The appearance of the light is also a sign. The sages have stated that the 'Brahmlok' is full of lights. It is a very fine sign. If this state is achieved it should be regarded as a blessing of Guru. The appearance of light at the time of sitting in meditation is also a wonderful thing. This indicates that the Sadhak has gone beyond the senses and mind and his kundalini is awakened. Some Sadhaks feel as if his seat (आसन) is raised up and he is sitting in the sky. Some feel that they are out of their body. Some feel vibrations and spasm in their bodies. All these signs indicate the progress of Sadhana. They should not be cause of fear. The breathing may be fast and the 'Istha Deva' may also appear. These different kinds of experiences, are not possible in every Sadhak at the sametime. The running of electric current and the shivering in the body are also good signs. In this experience the power travels to sahasrar and with a hard Practice the union with Brahma takes place.

If the Sadhak understands the reality and the siginficances of these signs he may march fast on the path of Sadhana. If neglect or disregard is shown the progress is sure to be hampered.

Swami Purushottamanand Tirth

LIFE

Swami Tirth was born in Vikrampur Daigone (Dhaka) in 1888, in a Brahmin family. Since his father was a yogi, he also developed interest in Yog and Bhakti since his childhood. He left his house at the age of 18, after having passed matriculation exam. Ramkrishna Paran-Hans house, was his mentor.

While a teacher, he was worshipped the photo of Shri Ramkrishna Paramhansa. RamKrishna used to say that who ever thinks of him he shall help him in uniting with the Guru. One day swami Purushottmanand saw shri R.K. sitting before him, in trance. He enquired what the samadhi was. Shri R.K. asked if he wanted to go into Samadhi. He kept mum. He said that he should make efforts. Saying this he (R.K.) sat on the shoulder of Purushottamanad. This made P.N. emotional (भावसम्पन्न). He started drawing when R.K. got down his form became that of Swami Narayan Tirth. Later one day while in meditation, he want into trance. He found that a woman with red apparel descended from heaven with a plate full of grabes and tried entering into his body. He become conscious with the sound of 'Hankar', and found his body trembling.

There was a Yogi, at Banotica a place about a mile away from his place. A friend of his asked PN to go to that Yogi. This yogi was none other them Narain Tirth, seen by him in dreams often. Narain tirth welcomed him and asked what kind of Sadhana did he do. He added that nothing is possible without the kundalini Jagran. PN requested him to allow him to live with him (PN). He agreed to do so after Proper test.

He went to him again after four from months. He saw some aspirants develop shivering during the Jap. He was highly impressed by this. In the morning Shri PN asked him if he wanted to be disciple. He said 'Yes', after thinking a while. He asked him to take bath and then initiated him. The year was 1910. When he sat for 'Jap', the guru asked about his experience. He admitted that while doing, 'Jap' , he felt as if something had ceased and the body started Shaking. After this he went home and meditated. He felt that a current flowed from the moolodhar to Sahasrar, his whole attention was deviated. He forgot the feeling of his body and enjoyed Himself great joy. During the 'Jap' he saw that there was a bright hallow around his head and with in that was the form of the Godess, created through Mantra.

The next day he visited his guru and he remained there for eight years serving him ardently. The very first day he went into trance just as he started jap and remained in that state for the whole night when he started 'Jap' in the morning he remained unconscious for three hours continuously. The kumbhak Pranayam started by it self. The guru asked him to stop the Jap but he thought that he had started it only a while ago. He again went into trance and sounds of different animals started coming out of his mouth it those of the Jackal and the lion. The world to him seemed filled with ecstasy. It was difficult for him to get out of that emotion. The Guru took him forcibly to dinner but he could not take anything. In this way he started experiences, asanas, prenayam, Madras and the movement of the Kundalini into chakras effort lessly. He recorded those experiences into a diary.

After sometime, he left for kashi and practised sadhana there like a Brahmchari. He lived for sometime at Rishiksh and Jhansi as well. He made a deep study of scripture of different kinds while in Kashi and wrote his famous book 'Sidha Yogopadesh or Yogvani', He wrote "Guruvani" and Jap-Sadhna, in Bengali, Lastly he took 'Sanyas' diksha from Swami Bharati Krishna Tirith, the Shankaracharya of Govardhan-radhadhish at Puri. As soon as he took guru Mantra and the guru placed his hand on his head be went into samadhi instantly. This, kind of Shakti transfer ceremony is called 'Sidhi Yog' in, Kularnav Tantra, it is called Bedh Diksha".

The importance of guru is great in the Mantra and Yog, Kriyas. If the guru is powerful and experienced, and the shishya too faithful and sincere, the success in this field in sure.

SIDH MARG AND KAIVALYA

'Sidhamarg' is that system of Yog where yog is possible without any difficulty or suffering. The path of 'Yogrup Sidhi' lies through Sushuramna. The pran Vayu, entering through this NADI, opens the way of yog, leading to the union of JIV and Brahma into the sahasrar. In the initial stage the guru opens this door and later the Sidh yog is had. The efficacy of Gurushakti awakens the kundalini, resulting into the attainment of yog. The yog-path is of two kinds.

(1) Natural and Artificial

The Natural is always comfortable and there is no harm or fear of any kind. Aganst this, the artificial or effort ful may cause difficulty. If the natural course is obstructed, there is trouble. Under the guru shakti all the Kriyas like Asana, Pranayam, Rudra etc are done effortlessly and unstrained.

If the 'Sidh Marg' achieved through Shakti-Sanchar, of the guru every activity seems easy and effortless. The sadhak dos not have to strain himself for them. A further March into this system, the realisation of the oneness of the jeev and Brahma, become easy, Therefore it is called Sidha-Yog.

When the kindalini Shakti soars up through the Sushumna marg the 'malas' (impurities) and the desires of the previous lives cause hinderance. The Shakti makes efforts to tide over them and consequently there is shivering and other kinds of vibrations in the body. Shikho panishad says.

"At the time of the soaring up of the Shakti the obstruction caused due to PranVayu, create may reactions. Shivering dancing, whirling, asanes do take place to cleanse the body. By this cleansing the Shakti reaches the satasrar and dissolves into Brahma randhra. The sadhak enjoys himself of deep samadhi. The sadhaks who have formerly cleansed sushumma, go into Samadhi with the rising of the energy at once."

Thus sidh-yog means the union of Chaitanya and the knowledge of the unity of Jeev and Brahma.

SIGHNS OF SHAKTI SANCHAR

The Shakti can not he seen with eyes but its play can be seen through the actions of the subject Kularnar Tantra describes that after the initiation many sighn's of shakti appear. They are the feeling of happiness, shivering, the asanas, hopping like a frog, sleep and trance these six are described thus :

"आनंदश्चैव कम्पश्चोद्‌भवो प्पूर्णा कुलेश्वरी।
निद्रा मूर्च्छा च वेधस्च, षडवस्था प्रकीर्तिता।।

It is of cource not necessary that all the six symptions should appear in every aspirant. Yog-shikhopanishad describes only, "Gatra Kamp," (Shivering of the body).

When there is no reaction or experience during the sadhana there can not be great zeal. As such, sadhana, without any experience or appearance is of no value. When the Guru Vakya, shashtra and self experience combine together the success becommes rewarded. The person who inspires shakti, is the real guru and the person who is inspired is real disciple. This kind of shrishya is treated like a son. Yogvashishta says:-

"दर्शनत, स्पर्शनात, शष्दात, वश्रया शिष्य दोहरे।
जनयेद्यः समावेश, शाम्भव सहि दोशेकः।।"

'One who is able to provide' Darshan Sparsha or Mantra, is the guru in the true sense. Kundalini, shakti Jagran and the Mantra Chaitanya are the same thing. Different Kinds of inter actions late place in the aspirant at the time of Shakti-Jagran on account of the obstraction of the former sanskaras.

Yog Shikhopani shad again adds:

"आधार वातरोधेन शरीरः कम्पते यदा।
आधार वातरोधेन योग्म नृत्मति सर्वदा।।"

"When the Shakti goes up, the pran, based in the Moladhar, is obstructed and varied reactions appear in the body.

HOW TO PRACTISE SADHANA

The Asana should be cosy one. Paṭansali yog shashtra says, "स्थिर सुखासनम्" | For Sadhana sit into any posture which is comfortable enough. In the next step, the memory of the guru should be brought forth in the mind. When the Guru-rarti appears candidly through meditation, he should he worshipped in the God form as the giver of knowledge and shakti. Then the name (Mantra) given by the Guru should be repeated. What further has to be done shall be known automatically. The Sidhamarg does not require any effort or Practice Everything occuers through the guru's grace. The Mantra Jap, does every thing. During the Jap, allow the body to react as it likes without causing any obstruction on the part of the sadhak.

Part Three
SADHAK KHAND

This part describes the experiences of the aspirants of the modern days who have had experiences similar to those of celebrated ones. The author narrates these experiences to inspire and enthuse the beginners in the field of sadhana. No age or time is unsuitable for the sadhana. Most needed requirement is to have complete faith and total submission. No effort of Sadhana goes without paying some dividend.

Pt. Trijugi Dayal Dixit

Pt. Trijugi Dayal was born at village Pipargoan in Farrukhabad district of up in 1915, in a reputed Brahani family. He had great regard for the saints since his boyhood. For sometime, he worked as a teacher in a local Middle School but later because a Panchayat Inspector. He got himself initiated by Swami Ramanand Maharaj in Syahi Devi camp in 1950. He described the experience of his first day Sadhana that his head had became hot. He felt like the piercing of needles. The body became heavy. His breathing increased fast and later stopped completely. He saw the light like that of the scene with of hallow. It increased by and by and his body became rigid. There was shivering and fast breathing and the fingers twisted into strange mudras.

The samething was repeated the nextday also. The other day he found his mooladhar hot. He witnessed a star like light before his head. He also had a sensation as that of the creeping of the ants in his mooladhar. He heard the hissing sound coming from inside.

He lived there for a week and had the same experience everyday. His guru at the time of parting blessed him by placing his hand on his head and patting his back.

While he was a teacher at his village school, he slept in the school instead at his home. He got up in the night and meditated in the mango grove by sitting near a well. He loved lonliness. I had some personal experiences during my own (authors) practice in 1953 and had regular occurrences of varied ASANAS and Pranayams and other yogic interactions. One day, while sitting in my room, I wished him that whatever has taken place in my case must also happen in the case of T.D. After sometime when I came back into the room he was in deep meditation. After that day various yogic and Tantric Kriyas started taking place by themselves even though he had only little knowledge about them. He was Panchayat Inspector then and I was a teacher at Dev Prayag. There was none to explain about his interactions but he consulted me through Correspondence. His Sadhana developed on and on. The history of the development of his Sadhana can be traced through his letters written to me at times which is as follows.

In his latter dated 21.12.53, he says:

"The work started at 6 in the morning. The work of awakening the upastha, Nabhi, heart chest, throat, brows, palate and the top completed. In the evening also the same spots here energised. The feeling of this 'Jagran' was felt by the current that flowed from the Mooladhar and energised all the other plexuses. The currents of power reached all the nerve centres through the help of the breath and it affected the nails even. It seemed that it did not leave even the hairs from being energiesed. When the Pranayam was complete I got tired. Then after the energising of the Mooladhar, samething pricked me like a needle and I felt an electric like shock. Thousands of currents of electricity seemed to pierceinto body to purify it"

"After performing various Pranayams, Asanas and Mudras in the beginning, I could not understand their significance. At that time the action of the purification of Mooladhar started after upastha. But Iailed because I did not know the process. So, I prayed to God and ultimately I succeeded in doing so thrice."

"The signs appear very slow and indistinct they have to be under your cautiously. There can be a danger too, if there occurs any kind of mistake."

IN ANOTHER OF HIS LETTERS, HE STATES

I sat for work (of purifriation through Kriyas) at about six in the morning. The mode and voice was a but different from other days the prayer was in the shape of a dialogue in the ordinary way. The Jap of 'Om' was also done. Suddenly I felt enveloped by an auspicious power. The old Kriyas were repeated and something new became my knowledge. The chakras of the previous day mere inergesed again. The process advanced. The work was begun by taking some soil into the hand (fist). The eyes were treated with the Anjun, (an ointment for the eye) like the moths does to the child. Tears of love trickled from my eyes. The teeth were also cleansed. The mother directed and I did likewise like a machine."

THE NEXT LETTER SAYS:-

"Many days have passed in repeating the Kriyas. All the centres are cleaned with the help of the breath carefully.

"The upasth and Mooladhar have different kinds of electricity which control the body. It seemed to me that the nose was the centre of all energy. The power energised all the muscular, nerves and the heir of the body."

"In the evening again the same process was repeated. The work of energising started. A pipe like sound was given out of month, with the gstures of the prayer with the hands. It was assoriated with song also. The words seemed to denote, "Chal Chal, Chali Aa Chali etc."

The power (शक्ति) sleeping at the Adhisther was swathistan. It awakened after a great effort, after invoking the mother. It started moving towards the legs. Efforts were hoverer made to take it upwards. It went up, after letting it listen to a sweet music of the flute. It raced up to Manipur and Anahat through Sushumma was slid down soon. This happened many times. It later rose upto the throat and refused to go on. It inclined towards the right and then to left arm. But the suggesdon of the mother refrained it from doing so. The tone of the shakti, changed whenever it changed its situation.

After ascending the throat the pattern of breathing also changed. I had to make hard efforts in this Kriya and after only complete submission the shakti rose upwards ultimately and it reached the sahasrar. In the first effort, there was not much trouble but at the second attempt there was some trouble. At the third there was perspiration and at the fourth it wearied me. It seemed that I might not die. I had to remove my hands from the nostrills by my own effort . As soon as I released the nose of my hands, the pressure of sushmma also decreased. I got up thinking that the work was complete. I thanked God, and the Mother heartily the whole night was full of great joy. I took some milk and went to sleep.

The next day, air was driven out from every centre by pressing them with the fingers. I had sat at five in the morning and the Kriyas could finish by two. They continued in the night also. When I aworke in the morning I felt quite blith and thought of the great success. I performed Havan and took my dessert.

"The day began with Pranayam. The nose was pressed with the thumb. I felt suffocated on breathing in. The perspiration started. As the shakti started to ascand, I started repeating Ram nam and asked others also to do so. It was followed by 'Onkar' the shakti reached sahasrar. All the outlets of possible retreat were blocked. The air was driven out through a special kriya."

"One night I dreamt that I was taken to some special place. On the wooden takhta, there sat a great person in white robes, with his face eastword. He seemed to be the chairman there several other persons were sitting on the floor. The great man declared, "Released," I bowed to him and returned. I becamse peaceful. It was all due to the kindness of Hanuman."

"This process continued daily. Daily the air was driven out. God Indra, made me drink nectar. Many other gods also visited."

"One day I went to bed after meals I felt that there was vibration in all the centres and the Shakti rose up. I pronouncel 'Onkar' and it reached the sahasrar."

"On the other day, the Kriyas took plarce by floating on the ground. Then, I was bidden to go on the kot. Many actions took place on the Cot. The nose-Bandhan was made and that enabled me to see devas. First Brahma, Vyas and next Shankar, with the Ganga flowing from his hair for several days the work of filling the body with air, and then throwing it and, continued. The inner Dosh (दोष) came out of my mouth for a number of days."

"Lord Krishna also showed his vision. He took his hand kerchief and made the knot of the nose, fast."

I felt that the shakti staying in the sahasrar, has been retained there with the help of Bandhas has. It continued hissing laudly. The skull opened and the air went out with force. I felt the outflow of the air, when I felt it with my finger I twisted my locks and with it, pressed the spot from where air was passing, Many Bandhas were also tightened.

The interactions continued after the sunset also and before the moon.

"Many twinkling stars, unseen before reached upto the moon. It seemed as if they were gods. They bestowed flowers and nectar. I was made free after the stars had reached the moon."

"When I got up at 3 am the Kriyas started again and they continued upto sunrise. I felt relief after their stoppage I visited the Hanuman temple and touched SHANKER and NANDI. I had an electric like effec. I asked my elder brother to put his hand on my head. As he did so, the shakti got down and became peaceful."

"I witnessed a snake with the jewel alongwith several other gods. I saw God also in the form of a golden image. I watched the dance of a very beautiful woman who was RADHA. Then I crossed over a bridge as thin as the spider Scam"

"One I felt that the shakti has entangled into SHUSHUMNA. I took many round jumps but it did not move upwords. My brother thought me mad and tried to tie with a rope. I got angry and returned home. Tired of the interaction I went to sleep. I rubbed warm ghee on my head and got some relief."

"The night of the full moon was rather wonderful. The kriyas took place peacefully. The shakti hissed loudly around the SHAHASRAR, through various orifices. Then it moved towords the Triputi I witnessed the figures of the sun, the moon, and panchanan Shiva. The shakti, then, entered into the face, the chest and into the whole body."

"I witnessed Ashwani Kunaras also. They made the Binoungs loose. Treated properly. They loosened the bandhas one by one. The Kriyas started again from three p.m.. The Ashwani Kumaras advised the massage of Mahanarayan oil. I also felt as if Vyas ji was Preaching on Vedanta."

"Inspired from within, I got my head fully shaven without leaving any hairtap. After this I had strange interactions. I retained faith in yogyopairt and changed it several times. On special occasions, during the Kriyas, I got off the yagyopavit. However put it on again after the interaction was oner. I took cold bath whenever I felt hot due to the shakti's arrival at the shahasrar. I took bath several times during the cold nights also."

" Once my tongue turned upside and struck into the palate. Many times I tried to reach my chin into the throat pit by sitting erect and moving my shoulders. This kind of Jalandhar Bandh took place usually. This stops the shakti from coming down. Many other bandhas were also used in the neck with the help of the hands. The Uddiyan and mool baudhas took place by themselves.

"The holes of the spots, through which the shakti had gone off, remained visible in the body for several days. A big orifice was made in the skull, through which the air passed off. The air also passed through the heart making a blowing sound. Many times it descended upto the thinghs and in that condition SHIRSHASHAN was resorted to, Another ASANA in which the legs were turned back to touch the ground."

"These interactions went on, sometimes for twenty six hours continuously. An interval was, of course, allowed. A new lesson started as soon as the former was finished when the Sushumna Pranayam was done, the air passed off through the month. When the air was inhaled, the sushumna mounted upwords towards the Shahasrar energing the chakras felling in between. It gave a great satisfaction. Lord Krishna presented a piece of his pitambar. A knot was made at the throat with that piece. Hanumanji put that Bandha, so that the shakti may not descend down."

"I felt like going into the sky along with a twenty year old woman. I came back after wandering with her several places. She was a goddess."

"Nectar flowed through the broken skull. It was very powerful, I took it into my hands and anointed the whole body. The shakti descended down while doing so."

"When the Rudra granthi was loosened in the Agya chakra I had a vision of the shiv Image having five mouths.

"I wished to look at the sun and came out of the room at 3 at the night. It seemed that the glimpses of the sun were coming out in the horizon. I had a deep took at the sun."

"I used to play to the mother sincerely. I felt as if she was coming towards the head making the sound of Onkar. Sometimes she produced that sound in the Triputi as a result of which tears trickled from the eyes."

In this way shri Trijugi Dayal witnessed different scenes and underwent many kriyas daily. Different asanas and mudras continued by themselves in. One of his letters later on, he wrote that the Kriyas had ceased. The teeth closed by themselves and air was inhaled with a hissing sound. He saw visions of many Mahatmas, one of whom was Swami Satyanand also. He blessed him and assurred success. Once I felt the presence of Lord Budha who seemed to say something.

Shri Trijugi Dayal have had long chain of experiences. His sadhana is still going on uninterrupted. But he does not want any show of himself.

Shri Sitaram Sajwan

Shri Sitaram Sajwan was born in 1956 in a village near Tehri. He passed B.Com and worked as a Govt. servant in HAL Haridwar. Initially he got initiated from Swami Ramanand in his Sukshma form and later from Sumitra Maa in Sadhana dham.

He inherited his religious feelings from his father. He heard him say in a vision that their path was the path of submission. Ram Nam is the only shelter. Sitaram replied that it might be suggestion of some well wisher. However, he started reciting Ram Nam devotedly. Soon experiences started taking place which he told to me regularly.

He had not read any book on Yog, neither he had association and guidance of any competent guru. He proceeded in Sadhana on the basis of his sanskaras of the previous life. The author (I) was very happy to listen to his experience. He removed his doubts and wrote down the experiences.

I had myself undergone such experiences and had read in books also and as such I had no doubts about them. It was rather my good luck that I had such a disciple. The following of his experiences may interest readers.

Relating to Shakti Jagran

"Some one from inside instructed me to sit in Padmasan. I sat in that posture for about 45 minutes like a stone image, without the least movement. The mind was peaceful and I entered the moolbandh easily. The nave thrust inside as if to touch the spine. The body straightened and the Chin touched the throatpit. All the three bandhas were perfectly on automatically. I entered meditation so deep that coming out of it seemed difficult. The breathing became very low. It appeared as if some power as soarning up from the Mooladhar through the spine. It reached shahshrar and got back upto trikuti. This going up and coming down continued for some time. Some times it travelled back to Mooladhar.

I felt that the sahassar contained lotus, Snake and a Shiv Ling. These three are the vital means of sadhana. The kundalini is like a serpent which lies around the shivling. It reaches Bhuling after soaring up to Sahasrar. The Swambhu ling are situated at both places the mooladhar as well as the Sahasrar."

"Sometimes I seemed that the Shakti leaving Mooladhar stopped at a certain centre. Here the thought and speech give way and only the existence of the Sadhan and Sadhya remains and they attract each other. What happiness is beyond description. One feels to live in that state for ever."

"It seemed to me that the kundalini was white and radiant like a snake and light was coming out of it. It goes up to Shiv, in the Sahasrar. Shivling is also very bright. The sahasrar possess the form of ॐ without Chandra Bindu. When the Kundalini reaches there, the Chandra Bindu also appears with ॐ."

"During the meditation I saw a white lotus with petals still closed. I entered the flower in my astral body form and set there like the blackbee (भौरा). There is profuse light there. I enjoyed myself great happiness in sitting there peacefully."

"Someone inside me, told that the Mooladhar is the place of Ganapati. I saw small idols of Ganesh there. I was told to remember them before starting Sadhna. The face of Ganesh was towards the back. I felt that the worldly people have their face on the front whereas the spiritualists have their Chetna on the back. The Chetna moves upwards through the sushumna situated in the spine. Therefore the Chetna lies on the back."

"I felt that a lamp was lit in the Mooladhar and its light reached the Sahasrar. As the bees surround a flower on its blooming similarly the Brahma Jyoti illumines the sahasrar. Several gods, goddesses, saints etc. gather around him."

"One day while in meditation I felt that Some one was dropping down a lunger (लंगड़) (a piece of stone, tied into a cord). It came down the forehead and went upto Mooladhar. There was a sensation in my nave. I saw the lunger, going down, with my physical eyes. I also saw, the sparks of fire, raining from the sky. The mouth was also giving out flames of fire and the whole body seemed ablaze.

"Some one from inside said that the Chakras help in the Soaring up of the Shakti in the same way as the parts of rockets do. I heard the sound of all explosion in every Chakra one by one when the Shakti entered them. The whole body was shaken by that explosion. The shakti reaches the sahasrar after exploding all the Chakras. Sometimes I felt that I was bathing into a waterfall, pouring down from my forehead. It was all light there. The current of shakti rose up making a gurgling sound. When it reached the nave, it gave a great jolt. The whole body shook. Another current of Shakti rose from the mooladhar. It went upwards towards the sahasrar, there it dropped down. This continued for many times."

"I felt that if the shakti alighted direct on the sadhak, his body shall not be able to sustain it. Therefore the help of the Guru is unavoidable. The guru allows that very extent of Shakti to drop that can to easily sustained by the sadhak. As the current of the Ganga could not be sustained directly by the earth, Lord Shanker had to have it on his head and then to release it slowly to flow on earth. Similar is the function of the Guru."

"Sometimes the Mooladhar produced sounds like the cracking of the finger joints. Somebody from inside, asks for Pranayam. And so the Pranayaṃ of that extraordinary kind that was never experienced before took place. With the shakti awakening different kinds of mudras of the mouth and the hands take place. These give ease and joy. Shivering, jolts, tears and thrills are all ordinary symptomes. The Nad (Sound) is heard day and night.

LIGHT

"Strange lights are seen during the night Between four or five in the morning, a brilliant light is seen that causes a break in the sleep. It is like the light produced at the time of welding iron Sometimes it is like the light of dawn."

"I listen an inner voice saying that you are neither body nor senses, you are pure light. Thus, the whole body became full of light."

"Strange things are seen before the Trikutee. It seems the whole atmosphere is wonderfully lit. The chandra Bindu of (ॐ) Shines into all beings as the kasturi lies in the nave of the deer. Formerly the light seemed to diffuse like that of the torch. Now it seems to focus at some particular point. That point is the lense of the eye. This is the self knowledge. This scene appears just at closing the eyes. Once at four a very strong light was focussed on my eyes and I was dazzled and stood up suddenly. The light seems to come from inside."

"During meditation the whole body becomes full of light. My Chetna, meditates upon that. Sometimes the figure (ॐ) becomes clearly visible inside the circle. One day, an atom of light was seen rotating. Sometimes it assumed the form of an iron ball. The colours of the ball keep shining. The vision of Ram and Krishna etc. Seen to appear in that ball."

"Once a point was seen rotating fast on the horizon. Strong light came out from the Agya Chakra like the light coming out of the rays of the sun falling upon a broken piece of glass. Sometimes dark blue colour appeared amid that light. Later the figure of god appears there. The apparel and the form appeared clearly.

"I feel the presence of a point of light within me. The Chitta reaches there. Then I became capable of seeing or listening anything. Every thing is done by resolue only. During the meditation the circle of light remains before. It contains beautiful images. They can he seen during intense dark. The light assumes the form of a point. This small point expands into a larger light. Out of mind all the things seem to emanate. In the night when all the lights are putout and I merge under the heavy quilt I feel the presences of bright light all around. This light is not warm, it is cool and soothing. It seems that a universe similar to the outside, exists within also. It has its own sun, moon, stars, planets and sky etc."

"It seems that I am sitting on a high mould and there is a point at some distance. A small light currant comes out from my head, it joins the point. The other point of base is also joined with that. It this way it complets a figure of right angled triangle. The ray of light that foms the diagonal moves, alongwith the movement of the point; ultimately the head point and the base point meet together. Only the right angle line stands. The headpoint and the base point are the sahshrar and the mooladhar. The Union of the two, creates the power. This power ascends through the sushumna. The ascending of snake gives me a feeling that I am also ascending."

"I saw a very radiant Shivaling, with an eye in the middle, full of blaze. The eye had a still brighter point inside. It seemed that the centre of all light was the middle portion of the brows."

"I saw a triangle like figure. A bright light like the noon sun was falling upon it. On the right side of the base, there sat a woman, wearing virmillion clothes, a copper ring in the finger. On the right, there sat a man with white clothes. The light fell on them from above. Both of them sat in a posture of meditation. I took a round and heard a sound saying. "Sharda. first I thought they were Brahma and Saraswati, the initiators of Brahma Kumari sect. Next. I thought that they wear only white clothes. Then I knew them to be Parmhansa Rama Krishna and his wife Sharda. Perhaps they were delivering some instructions to me."

From it all, it seemed that light is the supreme power. The whole universe is the procreation of that. God himself is light, therefore the hym. "Tamaso Ma Jyotirgamay." In the Ramcharita Manas, Ram has been described as Sachidanand DINESH (The Sun). The devotees pray to God as light and One. We all bow saying:

"ज्योर्तिमर्य जगदीश हे, तेजोमयी अपार।
परम पुरुष, पावन परम, तुझको हो नमस्कार।।

"Light gives the feeling of supreme power. Light pervades the whole universe. As the clash of the materials produces light similarly the clash of sounds creates light in the heart of man."

Experiences about astral body

"It seemed that an astal body has come out of my physical body in a diminitive form and has stood before me. Both the bodies are connected with a small stream of light emanating from my trikuti. A large lotus bloomed above my head, having a blend of white and red. I had a Shive Ling inside. It had three stripes like the three stretches of chandan (चंदन) light is coming out of the streaks. My astral body is impressing that I saw a tiger with open jaws but I did not feel afraid, I saw a python also with open month. Light was coming out of them both.

"My astral body reached the Himalayas soon. It offen reaches there. I meditate by sitting there. I come across with several rishis munis and tapaswis, with long beards. They bless and then the astral body resumes the physical one."

"It seems that several realised saints still penance in the Himalayas with their shukshma bodies. They conjuct their conscioudness with trees or block of stone and meditate during all the seasons of summer, rains and winter. They can assume any form by their resolve only.

"My astral body wandered into many spheres (लोको में), saw the scenes there, came back, and entered into my physical body. I was lying in Shavasan (सेवाशन) during that experience. The astral body while floating in the sky, felt like the everest that move smoothly. The astral body cameback as it had gone. On the return, usually, saints with white beards come across."

The Antariksha (space) is possessed by both the divine and devilish powers. The sadhaks are offen helped and guided by divine natured powers. These unknown powers help the sadhaks without any motive.

"Sometimes this astral body reaches the extreme limit of the earth's gravitation. The presence there develops the desire of being there when the astral body comes down, only then the memory of homes develops. Sometimes, there is a doubt about coming or not coming to the ground. Sometimes the astral body seems lying before the physical body.

Swami Satyanand says is his book Pravachan Peeyush: Some sadhaks have verbal or word expressions also. During the meditation also forms appear. Those forms appear with godly resolve. The visions and the advice inspire the Sadhaks. The soul, separating itself from the body causes reactions in the subtle nature and the Sadhak has wonderful experiences."

"I saw that my astral body was Soaring up into the sky. It reached a place where Swami Ramanand was Sojourning. Shri Ram Krishna and other great saints were with him there. It appeared as if a satpang was going on. I could discern it but dare not enter there."

"They took me to a cave where I could see the figures of saints. I reached a point of light which looked like a shivaling transparent made of Sphatik, about two inches size. Rays of light are coming out of that. In the round circumfrence Sat gods like Bramha, Vishnu and Mahesh, This circumference is increasing, continuing. Some unknown helper explained that behind the central point there is the causal point. This central point is radiant on account of the causal point. This Jyotiralinga is a radiation, many gods have been made out of that light. The whole universe is made out of that light. Eternal point is the source of all creaction, this is full of light and sound. As the seed so the first every thing is oval on account of that seed. Every thing will merge into the source that is Brahma."

This truth is based on all Scriptures. Bramha is the seed of all creation. It springs out of it and merges into it.

Once the unknown helper explained with the help of a figure drawn by it. This outer ring is your body. The inner is the astral body. When entry is made into the inner one. The outer one becomes useless. When the entry is made into the ring called causal one, the former two were reduced to no use. After that an entry is made into the forth called Mahakaran.

At that stage, all the former becomes one. This last one is the Adibindu which is soul element".

"We know that physical body is formed out of the five Koshas Gyanmaya, Anna Maya, Manomaya, Pranmaya i.e., and Anandmaya."

"At the close of the eyes, the Dhyan is fixed at that Atmabindu, the body does not exist during Dhyan. Only a point of light remains. I enter that and get dissolved. Both possess each other. The feeling of oneness appears there."

"The Shukma Sharir is floating into the sky. All the Chakras fell out of it one by one. The consciousness reached the Kapal (कप्याल). The body appeared like the bare skeleton. Then some smoke appeared and disappeared also. Only a point of light remained.

"I asked the inner guide as to what it all was. He told me that it was the truth which I was seeking. This is the soul element and this is the goal. After achieving this, there remains nothing unachieved. It is within you. The sadhana is the expression of that."

"After hearing this, the mind does not go after external worship or sadhana. I wish to meditate on that continuously. If the eyes are open , the sleep seems to overlay them. With the closed eyes I feel myself in a conscious state reciting mantra. The closing of the eyes has become habitual. The opening is effort . Geeta describes this state.

"या निशा सर्वभूतानां तस्यां जागृर्ति संयमी।
यस्यां जागृति भूतानि सा निशा पश्यतो मुने।।

"I sat in an Asan, meditated, the astral body came out and then breathing, but a light remained. That schemed to be Brahma.

"Now this unseen helper or inner guide asks to meditate on that. When one reaches the temple of Chandi Devi, the sight of Haridwar must be visible from there. There is no need of getting down. The meaning is, if the reality has been seen where is the need of asanas etc. every day, Meditate on that. All the things shall be left below, the things that were necessary formerly, now have become meaningless. Asana, Pranayam become useless. There comes a state in Sadhana, when external worship appears useless. Then the condition of "आत्मन्येषात्मना तुष्टः" appears".

During the meditation, the Shukshma Sharir, goes out of the physical body. But it is kept conjuncted with the pranic energy. If that is broken, death is inevitable.

The Shukshma sharir generally moves towards a snow covered Himalayan peak, of the shape of a trident. On the top, there is a circle of blazing light. The Shukma sharir moves towards that. It soars up after staying there for sometime. While soaring up, it comes across several gods and Siddhas. It reaches a place where a meeting of Siddhas is being held. It meets Ram Krishna, Arvindo and many other great saints. One day it saw Ramanad also among them.It can see them but can not enter the assembly. They converse and consult each other. The Shakshma Sharir reached up Gomukh. I wandered there in my smaller form. At a distances I saw a shiv Linga. Water is duping upon it from above. below is the Jabri (for collecting water). I offer Bel leaves on it."

Such kinds of experiences take place when the Sadhak reaches turiya state. A person standing on the top of the Himalayas can see the world, as well as the sky above. One can see the gods and the Sidhas but conversation with them is not feasible. They move, not with steps but slide out like the floating clouds.

Inner Divine Knowledge

Light is the supreme element. I asked the mother power how did she look after so many people. She retorted that the world was Hers. As there are parents to a child, similarly the universe has a creator. The Brahma is present in all sentient and insentient beings and all have emanated from Brahma. One becomes many and the multiplication goes on. Brahma is

Jyoti, light, the Supreme one. It enlightens every one. One may do good or bad in any concealed way, their knowledge goes to the creator who judges things. Brahma does nothing. The rays of light convey to Him the full account and the one suffers accordingly.

ऊं 'Om'is the power behind all the wonderful world and action. The point (बिन्दु) at the top, is not a point only; it is the third eye of Shiva. All the powers are hidden in it. The result of the maditation on ऊं can not be described. The secret lies in that point and it can be discerned by closing the eyes. When concentration is complete, the joy is beyond description

Kundalini: The wonder of the creation of this whole universe goes to the Kundalini power. This power living within human body, controls the whole body. This cradled figure is like the figure of ऊं. It is related to that and is like that in resemblance.

Someone says that you are not the body. It is nothing but light. As water is visible in the, ocean similarly light is discerned during meditation.

Oneness of Brahma

As the cows are of different colours but their milk is pure white, similarly human beings are varied but their soul is the same. The small seed contains the whole tree in the same way the whole man is contained in the semen atom, that can be held only on the tip of the needle. This small atom consists of the whole universe.

Tatwamasi (Thou are that)

The mantra comes out in the form of the words (TATWAMASI). The inner voice says that it should not be misused. The man must be evolved first. Taste the mango only when it is fully ripe.

Brahma can be realised

The inner voice said that Brahma can be realised. As the nose smells the odour of the flower, similarly Atman can also have Brahma. We can not see the odour but can feel it, similarly Brahma can not be seen but can be realised. Odour is the flower itself. The universe is also Brahma. While going to Delhi, we travel through the body like compartments and the soul like engine. After reaching the destination, the Atma merges into the Parmatma. As the sun is stationary and the earth revolves around it, similarly the Atma rotates around the Brahma.

The shakti seemed to say from inside "The one who comes to me sans desires gets much achievements. Who come with child like innocence get everything."

As there are many changes visible in naure before sun rises. It blooms flowers i.e., fragrant air begins to blow, waves arise in the rivers and the birds begin to chatter, similarly before the kundalini awakening many symptoms appear. Happiness of the heart aglows on the face, disconcern wih the worldly things, gentlleness, innocence, faith etc. begin to appear, interactions of different kind also take place.

Mother nature and her method

"The mother (power) teaches me like a child; as she wishes to take some work from me. She drew two triangles to explain that the life is a mixture of good and bad deeds. The good rise upside and the bad slide down. When their meeting point arrives, there arrives the state of God realisation."

"She drew another figure of a balance to explain that the two pans of the scale become balanced to indicate the state of realisation. She drew a third figure of a hexagon in which two triangles intercept each other to indicate the position of good and bad deeds. When the bases of the two triangles will meet the state of realisation would come. This state is described as "Shubhashubha Parityagi (शुभाशुभापरित्यागी) in the Geeta "This inner guide seems to me none other than the mother herself."

"Raag and Divesh (attachment and hatred) are the two great enemies. When I feel prejudiced against a man and I started denouncing him, the mother advised me that Raag and Divesh are enimical and they mar the path of Sadhna. They should be shunned completely."

"Different people with different natures take birth in defferent caste. A person born in a Hindu family is called Ravi Singh and the one born in Mohommadan one is called Mohamand Khan. The same Jeev born into different religions bears different names. Names also differ according to the place of birth. Therefore do not fight for names, places. The same God, is called Ram, Khuda, or anything else.

Submission:

"The inner guide explained when you travel in a car, you leave everything to the driver who knows the destination and takes you there, similarly whoever leaves things to me is led to the destination. Sow the seeds of charity in men and you shall be rewarded with much more.

"As there is darkness at the bottom of the lamp, similarly there is ignorance under knowledge. The maya is at the bottom and Parmatma always above."

"There are several circles, on one centre and the circumfrances have several points on them. Beings are sitting on them. Men are advancing towards the cercumfrance with their backs towards the centre. This advancement is material progress. Some people march towards the centre and they are sadhaks. All are apart from one another on the circufrance but when they move towards the centre, they all meet on the centre. Thus the arm of all religions is one. An urdu poet says:-

मजाहिब क्या है? राहें मुख्तलिफ हैं एक मंजिल की।
और मंजिल क्या है? जहां सब कुछ है, पर राहें नहीं होती।।"

"The answer to the question why man has to do Dhyan and upasana is that through them he acquries a magnetic power in him. This power attracts the divine powers towards him. The more a mantra is repeated or meditated upon, the more the magnetic power increases. The power makes his personality attracting."

"As to the question what defference is between Siva and Brahma, the guide explains that Shiv is part and Brahma, whole. As air filled in a ballon is a part of the whole air outside similarly the relationship between Siv and Brahma exists. Brahma is Sun and the Sun light particles are Sivas. Their element is the same. Shiv is in bondage and Brahma is free. Shiv is limited and Brahma unlimited."

"When the yogi reaches an advanced State, he rises above the difference of good or lead. His attitude towards the things of the world undergoes a change. He finds no differences between the mudding water and the water of the Ganga. Milk and wave are the same to him. His behaviour becomes child like. This change comes from inside."

Love for flute

"The flute has left itself to God and made itself fully empty. Therefore the voice of God comes out of it. When the surrendered person becomes egoless, he also becomes the flute of God.

"There is great difference between a Gyani and a Bhakta. There is a saying that the man bitten by a snake sleeps and the one stung by the scorpion weaps. Similarly the Gyani meditates silently and the Bhakta recites hyms loudly.

"Brahma weds Siva as the bridegrom goes at the door of the bride. Brahma goes to the door of the Siva and possesses it.

"The sadhak should consume himself like a candle giving light to others."

"There is the difference of 'karm' between the Bhakta and Bhagwan, otherwise the two are identical. The shakti explained that the world is like an ocean and I am swimming it. I can either swim or drawn my-self. The other course is to cross it, with the help of some one.

"Maya is like the shadow where Shiv is not. Maya is matter, Shiv is Shakti. Matter is Visible, Shakti invisible. The Jadpadartha (innert matter) is full of maya, having a shadow."

"Once during meditation the figure of a dark woman appeard and said that she was a divine being. I asked her to explain how knowledge comes. She said, through meditation. As an infant cries when it feels hungry and can not speak. So draws the attention of the mother for milk through it's cry. In the same way the meditation produces knowledge. The intense the meditation, the deeper the knowledge."

"The Sidhas and the gods balance the universe. When they feel unable they pray to God and God incarnates himself to do that.

"On being asked why Rama, killed Ravana, the inner voice replied that it was not Ravana, who was killed. The vices that caused disbalance, were removed. The pure Ravana, entered God."

"Why Shiva is bare while other gods clad richly? Lord Shiva clarified that the devotees pray barebodied. So in order to inspire them, Shiva also remains bare."

The secret of Samundra Manthan

The divine and the devilish powers Churned the occan jointly. This ocean is in our naval sphere, full of good and bad. If churned, it will produce fourteen jewels including the poison and the nectar, wine and woman. Shankar drank the poison without any evil effect. The poisonous snakes are his ornaments. The gods got the nectar. The awakening of Manipur Chakra, procreates everything. Churn it to get jewels.

In this way, the experiences are numerous. The lack of space, forbids me to stop.

Shri Umesh Narain Tandon

Born in 1965 in Meerut, Shri U.N. Tandon, passed B.Com. in 1988 and got initiate in Swami Ramanand Sadhana Dham, Kanakhal. Presently he is employed as a banker.

Speaking about his Sadhna he says that since his boyhood, he had an urge for seeking some unknown aims. One night he declared that he was going to Haridwar to stay there for sometime. Here it was the beginning of a wonderful change. As soon as he reached the limits of Haridwar, he was surrounded by some divine consciousness. He felt as if he were awakened from sleep.

He reached Haridwar at a very auspicious hour as the Spring Camp was going to take place soon. He sat at meditation and felt that new door was opened to him. The anguish that had gathered during the past, flew through the tears. Tears started flowing continuously for hours and the prayers of past time also found expression. He felt very light and happy.

The next evening a memorable event took place. As He was crying and praying, Swamiji came out of his picture and stood before him. He thought it a hallucination of his mind and continued praying. His heart was filled with deep devotion and it was the first experience of this kind in his life. A wonderful spectacle was before him. He put his head on the feet of Swamiji and then began the relationship between the Guru and his disciple. Swamiji made him stand up, placed his hand on his head and disappeared.

Then started the divine lilas. Soon he had the visions of Ram, Sita, Laxman and Hanuman. He started entering deep down. His head prostrated again and again on the feet of the Guru or Shri Ram. At last his prayer was granted and the Guru said, "Recite Ram, Ram, and his will be done". "On the next day I felt that Ram Nam was coming over my forehead. The relation of 'Ram Nam' conjuncted with the coming and going out of the breath. After five or seven minutes, I felt very warm. Afterwards my condition so changed that I kept reciting 'Ram Nam' even after Worship and Jap. I felt like reciting 'Ram Nam' loudly. I felt absorbed in 'Dhyan' even while attending Geeta or Pravachan class. The recitation went on while keeping awake and after meditation also".

Experiences about Shakti Jagran

The experiences of strong 'Shakti Sanchar' started from the very next day. The head automatically began to touch ground. Something seemed to creep in the spine from down to upwards. The Shakti spread into the whole body causing great joy. I wanted to lift up the head in the middle of the meditation. But it seemed to have stuck to the ground. After the bell of meditation, the force dimnished slowly and the head gained its original position. This interaction took place every time in meditation. Parekji later told that the awakening of the Shakti was very necessary for Sadhna and that my Shakti has awakened. Afterwards as the Shakti ascended from Chakra to Chakra, it appeared clearly. In the beginning it continued encircling the body for a longtime. The whole body was affected by it for twenty four hours. The Shakti remained active in the upper chakras first and then it descended upon the lower ones. Sometimes it rose from the lower to upper ones. It kept a balance between the lower and the upper. The supressed sanskaras appeared in the region in which the Shakti operated.

It was all surprising for me but I felt that I has under the influence of some unknown power. I submitted before that power completely and watched the activities. Once I prostrated myself at the feet of Guru. I saw the 'Ram Darbar'. These started flowing from the eyes and I submitted myself before the 'Darbar'. I heard a divine order that I should devote myself in the worship of Guru. One day I shall surely be liberated since I had gone into his care. Hearing that voice my tears stopped and I felt happy. The surprising thing was that the flow of tears was limited to me only and it did not draw the attention of other meditators.

"During one meditation, I had the vision of Ram in a serious mudra. Afraid, I asked the reason for this kind of mood. He said that I should worship Shwamiji before worshipping him.. I should recite the mantra of ॐ नमः शिवाय. He also said that he was associating his devotee Hanuman with me. Instantly Hanuman occupied my shoulder and remained with me continuously for three days".

"So far I did not believe in these scenes and thought that they were the imaginative creations of my mind. But God removed my doubts, himself. After rising from meditation my feet took me to the room of Shri Pareekji. I had no acquaintance with him formerly. Without hesitation I described to him the experiences of 'Ram Darbar'. He felt startled and asked me to describe the details. He exclaimed to me that such scenes could be witnessed only after a long Sadhana by the blessing of Guru.

Such scenes appeal before those Sadhak whose state becomes higher enough to reach astral spheres. The descriptions made in the Shastras are not false but every one can not see them. This meeting with Pareekji, confirmed my view that God, takes care of his devotees in the same way as a gardener takes care of his plants.

"In the morning meditation Ram, Krishna, Shiv and Vishnu appeared before me. The chakra of Vishnu released by him, came above my head and stayed. I saw Laxmiji delivering gold coins with her hands. I saw Brahma and Saraswati as well. Durga placed her hand on my head and touched me with her trident. The Trident is the symbal of power and its touch provided power to me".

"During the evening meditation, serpent with the jewel on its hood, appeared. The Jewel entered and disolved into the Jyoti of my heart. After that I had the vision of a Shivling made of grey coloured stone. On the one side there was Nandi and on the other was a Virmillion clad saint. He made me worship the 'Shivaling' properly. Two hands appeared out of the 'ling', from which streamlets of water flowed. Those sreams drenched us both. The 'Shivling' entered my heart through the scalp and disappeared".

His experiences continued even after the return from the Ashram and he wrote them down in his diary. I took notes from the diary whenever I went to Meerut. The experiences are worth a volume if published fully. Only the important ones have been described here. They are:

"I was initiated by Umadatta Laroia in the Ramanand Ashram. During the meditation Gurudev said that he had already taken the mantra before. Travelling back to Meerut, I remained in the meditative mood in the Bus. I saw that the Sai Baba of Shirdi appeared and sat on the bonnet along with other Gods. The divine one, blessed me. I had the vision of Ram, Shiv and nandi. The trident of Shivji was held by Ram and a light came out from the middle of it where the word Ram was inscribed. Vishnu sat on the left side of the trident and on the right was Shiv. Brahma was in the middle. The trident entered my body and its head touched my mooladhar. I had an inkling of Shakti in me".

"I was reading Ram Krishna Vachnamrita. All of a sudden my consciousness disappeared and I had an undescribable experience. The universal Mother appeared and stood between us and took me in Her lap and said "Lo, I shall satisfy your hunger of all the births". Saying this, she started feeding me with Her milk and in place of milk, Ram Nam entered my body".

I sat for meditation in the evening. After initial prayers Vishnu appeared with Laxmi. I paid my respects to both. Laxmi asked me what I wanted. I said your devotion. Then She took me to the Shore of the ocean. There was an empty throne and diamonds, jewels and arms were placed there. She asked asto what I wanted. I fell on the feet and said that I wanted only her grace. She replied in the affermative and took me up. Vishnu asked what had happened. She said that I had passed. After this my consciousness returned to normal.

"I was meditating, sitting in the temple of Oughar Nath (औथड़नाथ) A 'Pindi' came out of the original one and entered my body, announcing that it was in. The voice also asked me to meditate inside. After that Shiva and Parvati came out of the Linga and blessed me saying that I should go on like that."

"Just after initiation a light flame appeared in the heart region and my whole being was lost in that. After that, the flame continued to stay in the seven Chakras for many days. It appeared during the meditation and my being was dissolved. Later on I came to know that out of the many forms of God this flame of light is also one. Amritwani says, "God is light like".

"I sat for meditation at four in the morning. I saw Swamiji coming out of the painting and talked for a long time with Hanumanji. Then Shiv and Parvati came out of their paintings and took me with them for a stroll. After viewing the earth, they took me to the lower region (पाताल लोक). There I saw that the earth was rotatings on the point of a Shining Jewel. Seeing me surprised Shiv Ji said that the earth is a small playfield of God and is situated on a small part of his body. After this Shivji dropped his Trishul into me which had a burning light in the middle. He bade me meditate on that. He thrust the trishul into the Mooladhar and the mooladhar started stretching up. The same thrust down the chin close to the throat pit. The three bandhas became active. I saw Brama in the middle, Vishnu on left and Shiva on the right. Below them sat the goddess. The voice said that the Trishul was a symbol of God power. Brahma, Vishnu, Mahesh, Durga etc. are the parts of God. The only difference is that they have achieved Godhood while man has yet to aspire.

"I sat in evening meditation. The body became stiff, breathing stopped, the flow of Shakti started and all the external feeling disappeared. I regained consciousness after a long time. Ram came, alongwith Mother Durga. He asked the Mother to give strength to me. The Mother, replied that I was a good boy. I am watching him constantly. Ram said that I was full of devotion. The Mother said that my Mother was always shadowed by Her reflection. My mother shall be blessed. After this I regained my consciousness".

"I was coming to Meerut from Haridwar. I went into oblivion during the reading of Swami's book. I saw that Swami was standing with Ram Krishna. Ram Krishna put a garland around my necke that was wreathed out of while Jasmine flowers. On enquiry I was told that kind of welcome was given to all the new comers. Saying Swamiji disappeared into the person of Ram Krishna and both of them, disappeared into the Void. After that I had the vision of Hanuman. He opened his heart to show me the figures of Ram and Sita".

"In the morning, Shivji made me watch his dancing in the temple and said that one of his form lay in the idol of Natraj and the other playing upon the Damru. He should use a third form having the Third eye in the forehead. There was an immense flow of power and Shivlingas were visible every where. I merged into Shiv consciousness. He took me upwards and asked me to see downwards. There was all light like Deepawali and the Gods stood there. He, then asked me to sit down. My consciousness disappeared as soon as I sat. It came back after a long time. There I saw a cobra having white stripes on both temples. The cobra came to my neck and I felt myself Shiv like. I developed a beard and the current of Ganges started flowing. The sound of 'Shivoaham' was heard all around".

The recitation of 'Ram Nam' goes on continuously. In the office also, when I had a nap, the inner string joined with the spirit and I saw that 'Brahma' was sitting on the naval lotus. Now, I felt that the power, which was called 'Mother' by Ram Krishna, operated in the body also. That very power is worshipped. The worshipper thinks that he is worshipping some power sitting outside in the idol but in reality, the Mother sitting inside is worshipped. The supreme father makes the worshippers sit in his lap and a flow of strong power starts. Ram Krishna said that he talked with the Mother like a living power. My condition was also the same. On prayer both appear before me and we have a long conversation."

"I was sitting in the temple. I saw Ram Krishna sitting on the 'takhta' outside the room of Sumitra Ma, alongwith Swamji. Ram Krishna asked as to what kind of Sadhana did I want, Vedic or Tantrik. I said the one I could easily proceed on. Ram Krishna and Swamiji both disappeared after saying 'Al right'. Next time Swamiji appeared with the Kamandal in his hand and asked me to take water which was very clean. I started drinking it. Swami advised that I should leave some for others also. He was pouring water while I was drinking. Some water outflowing through my elbows and some woman was drinking it greedily. Many others also drank through that woman. There was a crowd gathered there for water. I saw Sumitra Ma, walking in the verandah alongwith my grand parents. They pointed to Sumitra Ma, walking in the verandah alongwith my grand parents. They pointed to Sumitra Ma, that I was their grant son. Then she nodded and blessed instantly, a flow of power started into my body".

"One day during the meditation, I reached Gyanganj where Vishuddha Nand had acquired divine knowledge. All the saints present there, disappeared and only I remained. I saw a golden fort into which I vainly tried to enter. I woke up soon".

"One day some 'sanskar' was causing trouble. Swamiji appeared and consoled that I should not worry. I lay into his lap and he patted me like a child. I found it difficult to get out of the meditation as the bell for meals had gone. There appeared vivekanand and advised not to bother about what people say. There should be first resolve and aim before. Let the people say as they please.

Once during meditation Durga, Saraswati, Ganesh, Kartikeya, Indira etc. appeared out of the photo of Swamiji and entered into my body. Many times Om in the written form appeared and disappeared. I saw that I sat on some chakra yantra which had settled on a city. This Chakra was radiating the sound of 'Ramnam' and the people below were being affected by it.

"Guruji came and took me to the temple of a goddess and asked me to pray. This event happened as some sadhak's thought that swamiji did not believe in the god and goddesses. This idea was within me so whenever the figure of some deity appeared in meditation, I ignored it. On a request for guidance in this matter, swamiji took me to the temple himself. He explained that the aim of Sadhana was the realisation of God who manifested in the deites also; so, none should be ignored.

"Lord Krishna let loose his Sudarshana Charakara which came and hovered around my head. I went back into the hands of Lord Krishna but the bright rays radiated from the Chakara surrounded me. After this my mother temper was lost and that of Lord Krishna became dominent. The Chakara came into hand. A sensation continued in the forefinger even after that Bhav (भाव) had disappeared. I also saw Krishana standing on the earth playing upon his flute. My consciousness was driven to his feet and merged into Krishana. The whole world appeared but like a toy. Every thing seemed to rotate. I saw Hanumanji sitting on a temple and throwing rose flames on the sadhaks. A flower struck my head and my Sahasrar energised soon and filled me with happiness.

"While meditating at the feet of Swamiji, I enter into the subtle state and canverse with swamiji like a son to the father or a disciple to the guide. One day Swamiji took me to the river and we were transported into big and small fish respectively. He said that there were many disorders on the surface therefore we should go into deep 'Sadhana.' One day Swamiji was sitting on a chair, I touched his feet. He made me sit on the half chair, we transformed into one. There I saw many 'Sadhaks' sitting there. My consciousness disappeared and it came back after a longtime. One day I came to the door of the Hall in the apparel of a bridegroom. Swamiji appeared out of the photo and garlanded me with the words that from that day, we were wed together. I took it as the union of soul with God."

"Once I thought that most of my time is spent in office work and during working hours I forget about God and Guru both. The same day while I was taking tea at 11.00 a.m. my eyes closed and I heard Swamiji saying that it was not proper to say that I forgot him. He was in my soul. I appear here as a proof of that."

"Sometimes the astral body goes on the tops of the hills, feeling great peace and joy. On some other occasion, the body enters an aeroplane which takes me to a higher abode. The body begins to radiate currents of 'Ram Nam'. My consciousness passes on England where the sound of Christ and 'Ram Nam' are heard. It flies over Makka also where the sound of Allah was audible. All this proved that the same power was residing everywhere."

"Ganeshji arrived and made me sit on his rat van. After sometime the rat went away and the consciousness started up rising by itself. After sometime the consciousness was gone and only a point remained. That too, disappeared into the sky. A voice said that the point was the causal body and it merged into the grand causal."

"So far I had witnessed only one aspect of Sadhana, i.e. the visions and appearances of devas, sidhas etc. In the other aspect the vices go out of the body. The journey of Sadhana appears like the journey through the vales."

"As a result of this Sadhana many inner and external changes have come. Attachment is decreasing and a feeling of happiness is increasing. Everyman now seems a soul. The external actions appear like acting while the reality of inner working seems proper and real."

"I watched in the meditation with there was a small boy with Swamiji, only half clad with a dhoti, head shaven, and wearing 'Yagyopavit' Swamiji also was clad like the boy. The boy seemed to me like my younger brother. Swamiji took him to a temple."

"I had several experiences about the Shakti. The Shakti reaches into the body and changes take place accordingly. In the beginning the flow of 'Ram Nam' inspired Shakti as has been explained in the 'Amrit Vani':

राम नाम पद शक्ति जगावे ।
सुधारस सींच शान्ति ले आवे ।।

"The grace of the Guru, energises the Kundalini Shakti. The 'Ram Nam' Combines with the breathing. This 'mahamantra' conjuncts with the Shakti. The awakening of Shakti is related to Shiv and Shakti. I saw that a trishul entered through the Sahahrar and its lower portion touched the mooladhar. The mooladhar seemed to go up. The nave streched towards the spine. It eased after sometime. One must know that any state in Sadhana is not permanant. Every thing keeps changing. When the recitation of 'Ram Nam' goes on, the Waist seems to bend. All the bandhas open and the head touches the ground. The flow of Shakti becomes so powerful that it does not become possible to lift the head."

"One day, as soon as I sat in the morning Mudras started taking place. The Shakti Chakra came out of Sahashrar and entered the mooladhar. I lay down and did not know what happened afterwards."

Kriyas for Shakti awakening :

"Whenever there is any hindrance in the rising of the Shakti above, many interactions take place in the body i.e. the turning of the neck, clapping or dancing with joy. Different pranayams start by themselves. The breathing becomes fast like the hissing of a snake.

Hit on the Mooladhar

The breath was hitting the Mooladhar like a hammer. It became soft after sometime and it later seemed that it had stopped completely. The body became still. After meditation, I lie in Shavasan (शवासन) and become unconscious. Then I hear the sound of loud clapping. These reactions remove the stiffness of the body. The stomache thrust in and meditation on the Triputi become easy.

The interactions of the awakening of Shakti take place in various ways. The breath grows fast, the head droops on the earth. The Shakti ascends up. The Sadhak sees the flames coming out of the Manipur and also the Sushumna, soft like the thread of lotus. One day, a coloured cobra appeared during meditation. It descended into the Mooladhar and then ascending from there, reached the Sahashrar. This Kriya continued for days.

"Once a lotus bloomed suddenly, I entered in to that fully conscious. There was no breath yet the petals opened and I came out. One day a lotus flame bloomed in the Sahashrar. The Shakti rose from the Mooladhar and reached the centre of flower. The lotus closed and instently my neck droped down. I became conscious. This happened many times. As the breathing stops the three Bandhas take place. After their easement the force of the sound of 'Ram Nam', affeets the mooladhar. The Shakti is seen ascending up".

"One day, while sitting in meditation the breathing became fast. The PRAN rose up. A light was burning and the chetana was looking at it. The flame of light fixed itself into the Sahashrar and the whole body became resplendant with blue hue."

"One day a current of water light emanated from the hand of Swamiji. It enwrapped me fully. The breathing stopped. There was a pressure in the Triputi. It contracted. A flood of blue light filled the atmosphere. It seemed as if another door had opened for me."

"When the Shakti interacts at the 'Swadhisthan Chakra', many amorous scenes appear. There is a strong possibility of the fall of the Sadhak. But he overcomes all, with the help of 'Ram Nam'. I saw many beautiful maids dancing lustfully. I was made to sit in the court of Indira. Many temptations were given. I was troubled in the beginning but everything was over soon. When the Shakti started working at the Mooladhar, the lusty desires appeared. But afterwards the mind became pure and peaceful. When the Shakti worked at the 'Agya Chakra' the thoughts of very high order appeared. The Shakti rises up by expressing the special characterstics of that Chakra.

The path of Sadhana is very strange and can be realised. Different experiences can only be felt. They can not be described through words. There is no power to do so.

Deo Prakash Gupta

Born-1950 in village Budhai Purwa Dist. Gonda (U.P.) Education BSc. Initiation 1986 Sadhanadham, at present collection Anim Farrukhabad.

As a consequence of Diksha, the spiritual seeds lying the heart-land germinated and flourished with the success in Sudhana inclination and courage developed slowly. He got a new direction in life. There was a tremendous change in the behaviour and nature every part of life illumined with the colour of spirituality.

He started sitting in meditation every evening and morning. He reported his experiences sought suggestions and wrote them in the diary. The path of spiritual evolution opened before him. The description of these experiences is made below.

Light : When I look in the darkness, with closed eyes, light appears there. The same light is visible on opening the eyes. The colour changes. It is sometime white like silver sometime yellow or blue. These colours are so attractive that their chain becomes beyond description.

ANAHAT NAD

"Sleep ended at 2 in the night. Started the Jap of Ram Nam. The sweet sound of NAD was being heard. It was akinto the sound of the Crickets. It was rhythmic and sweet. After that strong rays of light appeared. Some unseen power asked me to go up. I stood up in my astral body and started floating in the sky without fear. The shakti was guiding my course. After sometime I came back into my physical body."

"Got up at three as usual and sat for meditation. The NAD was sounding highly. After sometime the ball of light appeared. It seemed as if some shakti has entered my body. Many kriyas were taking place inside. I was lying with my knees bent. I was advised to unfold the legs. AS I did so, the interactions increased. I was slightly afraid. I prayed to Guruji and the Kriyas ceased. The Jap and the NAD was as before lying there I feel as if I was running. After sometime the advice came to stretch the legs. I obeyed and prayed the mahashakti to lead me through an easy course. The chant of Ram Nam had covered me fully. The whole night was spent chanting Ram Nam. On awakening in the morning I feel happy and peaceful. Thus after I witness the ball of fire during mediation and heard the celestial sound.

"In meditation, I saw a snake of dull colour killed and crushed by some one. It started imning after sometime and because alive and active. I felt that I was endowed with some power and I could go any where in my astral body."

"While meditating in the night, it seemed to me that some power was bending my head forcibly. My head touched the ground . Gradually I got into sitting erect many. Kriyas were going on inside. I was feeling the upsurge of the shakti into different chakras. They were working beyond my control. I was simply witnessing them."

CERTAINTY OF SHAKTI JAGARAN

"In the morning meditation, I saw the shakti rising up from the mooladhar and reaching the head. The head touched the ground and the rosary fell off. I prostrated myself at the feet of the mother and thanked for the grace. I requested the mother to he kind to me who was an ignorant and innocent child. Different interactions were taking place and I did as I was told. My chin touched my neck which was Jalandhar Bandh. I was hearing the rhythmic sound of a gong like the one that is sounded in schools. After meditation. I felt light and happy."

"I was chanting Ram Nam. I felt numb soon. The whole body became numb, the forehead touched the ground. It seemed that some divine being sprang water on my head in order to bring me to consciousness. Instantly some power separated my astral body from the physical one. I felt a light shock. I was quite unnerved. I felt as if I was completely naked. I aspired higher and higher in that condition. After sometime I came back into the physical body. I felt great peace. I sat in meditation hearing the Anahat Nad. I chanted Ram Name. The breathing increased and terned into Bhasrika Pranayam. It continued for sometime then the breath was reduced to nil. One hour passed in this way. I lay in shavasan and meditated. I felt gain and again that I was being carried up and up. I prayed to God saying that I did not deserve it. My sails were in his hands. I felt then the presence of some saints in the space. I prayed to them I felt that I was being dragged towards them. This position was very pleasant. I came back to my physical body after sometime."

"After meditating for one hour, I lay in Shavasana. The Shukshma sharir separated from the physical one and started floating into the sky. I saw an AGHORI BABA there. I approached him and respected him with folded hands Gradually a shivering started into my body and I started flying up. The gusts of winds touched my body. I felt a little uneasy. The chanting of Ram Nam became fast. I came back to my physical body after sometime. I heard a loud voice saying that it had taken me in its possession. I was impatient. The ball of light came before me. I felt very happy to look at it. I offered pranams to my Gurudev repeatedly."

"I saw shakti rising from my mooladhar and going up towards the sahasrar. It seemed as if all the Kriyas were being done by that. The Uddiyan Bandh took place and nave seemed to touch the spine. Mool bandh was also on. I meditated lying in shawason. The whole atmosphere was filled with light. The sound of Nad was so fierce that the ears seemed to burst. The condition subsided after sometime."

"Today I sat for meditation at 4 a.m. The interactions started soon. I was following the intuition. Later on when I read the yogic books, I found them proper. They proved very useful in shakti Jagran."

"Now when I sit for meditation many kriyas start in the body and pran. Different kinds of Asanas, which were unknown to me started laking place. They made me very peaceful. A new kriya started just after the one ceased. These Kriyas started just after the one ceased. These Kriyas removed my fatigue and developed interest in Dhayn."

"I lay in shavasan and my Shukshm body reached the Sky. It started revolving round a centre. I was clapping and chanting Ram Nam. I thought that all this success could not lead to Bhagwat Darshan. I became emotional and started weaping. God heard my player. God appeared before me in the form of a strong light. I prayed reverently. God asked me if I felt hungry. I did not feel any want at that time. I said that I had no desire at all. I was fulfilled with the grace of God. I thought about the people who doubted the existence if God. I saw personally how kind he is when my consciousness returned, I thanked the unseen power again and again. Such experiences occurred to me again and again. Whenever I flew into the skey in my shukshma body I felt highly elated.

"With the grace of the Mahashakti, I flew in the sky like the birds. A felt a little fear while coming down but there was joy also. I prayed to Mahashkti to permit me to go down. I dropped my head at the feet of the mahashakti. She took me in Her lap and patted me gently saying that I should drink warm water. She fondled for a long time and after that I reached into the physical body. My kriyas start as soon as I sit for meditation. My chin bends down by it self and the teeth clench. It is all done by some power on which I have no control."

"I wake up at three in the morning without any lethargy. I get up, wash my hands and face, and start meditating. This practice has been going on since my intation in the Sadhana Dham, Kaukhal. When I sleep at home, I meditate for two hours daily. When I sleep in the night, I always look for the morning to come and meditate and enjoy myself the divine bliss. Similarly I want for the evening. Day and night. I hanker for the bliss."

"Today morning, I went into Uddiyan Bandh, as soon as I sat in meditation. The room was closed from all sides but there was divine light there. When I close the eyes, the light appears and when I open them, I see darkness."

"Today, I reached a sphere where there was darkness alone. I continued chanting Ram Nam. After some time, I regained my original state."

"Sometimes I saw lord Krishna enacting leelas like a boy of eight years." Sometime I become quilt numb. I lose all the feel of the body. The body becomes heavy so much that I can not move it. At othertime I become light enough to fly easily into the air. Sometime I enter into samadhi state and forget who I am and what is the time. I only feel my existence and often I lose that sense also.

Shrimati Sadhana Singh

Born at Meerut in 1965, Parents very devout. Education: B.Sc, B.Ed Initiation 1989. Husband Shri Sanjay Singh of Lucknow.

The door of experiences opened after the initiation. Some of the experiences were narrated to the author of this book. She started them in writing on his insistences. The grace of the Guru, Saints, Gods and God rained upon her:

जा पर कृपा राम को होई।
ता पर कृपा करें सब कोई।।

Some experiences, regarding her sadhana are detailed below in her own words.

"I saw that Ramayan was going in a large garden. Long queues are there at the time of Arati. I think that I shall get no chance. I go into the temple where Gurudev is standing on the stage bearing a tired look. Addressing me he says that he is tired of standing there so he wants to change the body. He asks me to go to him for support alongwith another Gurubhai. He stands up by placing his hand on our shoulders. He descends the steps and vanishes. I run fast to hold him up".

"Mother Mariyam comes with a child in her lap. She drops the child into my fold and vanishes, I feel the presence of Christ soon after".

"An event of my past life reviewed like the cine pictures. My marriage has taken place in some Royal family in my childhood. I come out by giving up his hand. Then I see a woman in white clothes. She asks me what I was doing there. There are dacoits outside. We should hide in the temple. On coming out of temple, I see many dead bodies lying there being killed by the docoits. I am alone. My husband has become a sanyasi. I look after the state. I become old and enjoy respect of the people. I go for bathing in a river. I drown and die".

They bowed arround my body and at last entered into it.

Chaitanya Mahaprabhu, alongwith his devotees, is coming on the road. He put three scarfs (चुन्नियाँ) on me and placed 'sindur' on my forehead.

I saw a shivaling with a bull sitting beside. It was told that a temple should be built there. i sat there, stupefied.

The Swami gave bouguet and it turned into abrush. He asked me to apply colour with it. Mother Kali blessed me again and again.

Nanak appeared and placed me into his lap like a child, put a garland on my neck and asked to repeat 'Sat Nam' Sat Nam".

Ram Krishna gave me pudding to eat. I devowred it, placing the cup at my lips. Sitting in meditation, I had an electric like feeling. The body thrust backward as it to lie. I lay flat. Both the hands were stuck to the earth. The face made mudras variously. Some power made me sit. My mouth parted more and more. The eyes stayed open like the god-image. The goddesses began to bless. The head tossed back, the tongue uplifted to the palate and, I entered Kechari mundra. It seemed as if the body had touched the roof. It came down, the mouth opened and the tongue dropped. The body trambled and the tongue watered. These Kriyas continued for several days.

After physical kriyas the internal started. The eyes closed completely and the centre of the forehead seemed to flutter and a flame like that of a lamp appeared in the middle of the forehead. The blaze increased so much that the consciousness was lost. In the beginning this condition lasted for seconds but later it increased to minutes gradually.

The sense of time was lost even. My sookshma body hovered in the sky. Many wonderful scenes appeared forming into stars, mountains woods, etc. These were beyond description.

The Mooladhar stretched upwards and the nave went down. The stomache tried to touch the back. I would not stop. The interna, power did it all. It seemed, some power was taking upwards. The teeth closed fists cleanched and the face had a green look. It seemed to burn and burst soon.

A light emanated from the triputi and spread into the whole body. The body lost its feeling; only light remained. The vision of Sidhas and deities, appeared.

"While in meditation, it seemed that a very old sage had awakened from meditation and was proceeding towards the heart. He inspected my heart as a person does before boarding a boat. He came out of me and then went in his sookshma body. After this, it seemed to me that all the actions of walking, talking and eating were done by him. My face also changed like that of his".

"Sometime, I felt that a circle of light was hovering over my head.

Whenever my gaze stopped, that object was surrounded by a hallow. Sometimes it seemed that the shine of my eyes, made other object, shine".

"I was going through the diary recording the experiences of others. Immediately I heard the bell go. I closed the diary and sat thinking how high the experiences of these people are. They have the visions of higher order due to their Sadhana. Thus thinking I sat for meditation. I heard my Gurudev say that these experiences were of no avail to me. Your's is the path of Bhakti, proceed on that. Then I felt as if my hands were extending for getting something. I never knew what it was but most probably it was bhakti itself".

"Whenever I am alone, I have a keen desire to have the darshan of God or Guru. I feel like a mad man. Tears do not stop, the throat gets choacked, the lips wet, I begain to dash my head that makes the forehead swell. The only idea, that I should have the vision of God, haunts me".

Once I felt that a large snake has eniwrapped my nack and its' hood is on my head". "I saw the goodess sitting on lion emerging out of the photo of Swamiji. She disappeared in the Shivalinga yonder. The Shivalinga entered my body".

"My neck seemed to have light in the upper part. The light discended and reached Muladhar. The whole body got lit".

The Veena Goodess clad in white appeared and entered my body. I saw Kali, with the garland of Skulls and she put that garland around my neck.

I saw the lighted OM (ॐ) with rays bearing the inscription of 'Ram Nam'.

I was in meditation. Many painters appeared with brushes. I asked on whom they were to be applied and where the varnish was. The Swami answered that there was no need of varnish. These are cleaning brushes only. I said that I did not know how to clean. The Swami said that he will do it himself.

I saw a large Shivalinga, filled with dazzling light. There were many snakes there.

Ram, Krishna, Vivekanand, Ramanand, Shankaracharya and Sai Baba of Shirdi were prominent. For some days, the word Om (ॐ) appeared with the light Om to blow in the sky even with open eyes. Sometimes it seemed that Saraswati had entered the body. Gurudev Ramanand appeared in the form of Christ. He had made the gesture of reading 'Ayats' and the head bent in 'Sizda'. Sometime there seemed to be the obsession of being Devi and the body zoomed. Sometime, the body begain to Spring like Hanuman. Then, the eye flooded with tears for days together to have the vision of God. There was uncontrollable laughter sometimes, and it continued for a long time.

During all these interactions, the body got hot and the hand, moved from up to down automatically. The flow of energy was so great that the head bent down to touch the ground. As the head, touched the earth, strange kind of rays emanated. I felt circling in the sky like the stars on their own exises. I felt afraid then but after sometime everything became smooth. I felt as if all the parts of head have opened.

I was reading 'Ram Krishna Leelamrita', when the context of giving of initiation in Vedanta, by Totapuri came, the book slipped from my hand and there was the fast descent of energy on my body. The mother laid me in Shavasan and I became unconscious, when the conscionsness returned I heard someone say that the recitation of that mantra was necessary for deep Samadhi. The time during the unconscious state appeared to be very small but the watch told it to be more than an hour. I knew nothing of the happenings taking place around.

The feeling of Motherhood increased so much that all appeared like my own children. Even, the emotion appertained to parent. The heart seemed filled with so much mother affection that only God. Mother could control it. Lord Christ also has accepted me his mother, while I sat in meditation he offered the garlands. I protested and said that my place was under his feet. He said that I was mother and my place was in his heart.

While I go to Dakshineshrar in Samadhi awastha, Ram Krishna offers me pudding in a leaf plate, already partly eaten by him.

I saw in dream I have gone to the Hanuman temple. As soon as I sit to meditate, the idol makes me Samadsiptha.

All the Chakras begin to vibrate and open with force. I feel stupefied completely, unable to move. People looked at me with wonder at that time my dog came and chased all away.

Goodess Kali appeared in Samadhi and stood before me. I felt that I was kali myself. I saw her figure and found that there was the difference of only arms. She had eight and I only two. I embraced her irresistably. She also embraced me throwing away all her weapons. I felt like the touch of thousand lightnings. Even today, the memory of that experience thrills me.

I had several experiences of this kind. Once I saw Parikji preaching. I was listening to him attentively. I saw a sound of hallow arround him. A wave came from that and entered my body. This was repeated a number of times and lastly the force was so great that I became unconscious.

Once on the concluding day of Sadhana camp on full moon day, at the time of Arati. I saw Gurudev coming with his usual smile. I offered flowers to his feet and he blessed me. He was followed by the visits of Ramkrishna, Satyanand, Sumitra Ma and Parikji. I was told that they all were appionted to guide me. I saw the real form of Gurudev in Parikji. In dreams in the night, Swamiji appeared again. I worshipped him with flowers and touched his feet. Tears of gratitude came to my eyes. He started giving me instructions. I got awoke soon, and felt my body electrified.

When the Sadhana was in full bloom I was always intoxicated with pleasure. I did the work but felt that some one was doing. I was surprised. Whenever my eye was fixed on some objected, it disappeared leaving a light only. God seemed in everything. The same light was every where and within me too.

Shri Rajesh Narain Tandon

He was born in 1971 in Meerut. The home atmosphere was of worship, jap and God discussion etc. Passed B.Com. and sought initiation in 1989. His occuption is business. He came to Kanakhal in 1989 and stayed with me for a week. Got initiation by Laroiya Ji and proceeded on the path of Sadhana.

He was so much engrossed in the Guru Bhakti that he reached Digoli, the place of Sadhana of Swami Ramanand. He became deep rooted in Spirituality. The sadhana camp made his resolve firm. He started experiences and his out look to life completely changed. Sleeping or working his only urge was to achieve his aim of Sadhana.

Following are some of his experiences that have been extracted from his diary on 23.4.1989. He wrote in his diary.

"I experience a voice coming from within and explaining to me about my experience. I also feel that the influence of Swamiji remains with him while meditating. He inspires through his power to proceed on the path of Sadhana. I have started writing them out, without ignoring them".

"On 14.6.1989, I sat for Jap. I closed my eyes and became devoid of thoughts. I saw the rising sun with it's red rays scattering everywhere and reflected into the river water. I felt as if I were born a new. A host of god's seemed to bless me by placing their hands on my head".

"One day I saw a circle of light, hovering before me and then disappearing. On another occasion, I saw the light of a lamp just at closing my eyes. It also disappeared soon".

Once I saw Swamiji with a trident like that of Lord Shiva. He thrust it into my breast which became red with blood. But it appeared as if the 'Ram Nam' where written there.

On 23.4.1989, during the Jop, I saw an image of Budha, precaching peace to me.

The round circle of the sun appeared. On close watch, it revealed the word of Mother, written inside it. On the otherside was the name of Gurudev. I invoked the Mother and a light appeared before me, like the third eye of Lord Shiva.

I found myself, sitting in a temple, besides the idol of the Mother.

Rays of light, came out of her hand and they entered my body. Mother had a rosary in her hand and that turned into a Loket with the picture of Swamiji. The Mother seemed to enter into that. I called Mother! Mother! emotionally. I thought when Mother will pervade, no attachment shall exist.

"Sitting in meditation I found the blue sky throughout bubbles, of different colours. I saw them and realised that the Sky is God, everthing is coming out of it".

"During the Jap, the sound of 'Ram Nam' increased more and more. My body also vibrated with its motion,. I kept reciting and laughed; eyes filled with tears. It was all prompted from inside. If tried to check, it caused grief and it'sad vent gave Joy".

Once I found myself stood in a great hall of the church. Candles were lit on all sides. Some prasad was placed in the paper plates. Every plate had a cross on it. I was filled with the memories of Christ and felt elated".

I read the books of Ram Krishna. While I sat in meditation, I found myself reduced into a child. Many women are standing before me to feed. One of them, took me into her lap.

I prayed to God that he should occupy my body completely preventing anyother thing from entering my body. I wished no worldly joy nor sorrow. His will was all. I thought God to be my mother. Thinking these thoughts, I got my throat choked given expression only to the words, 'Once you, only you'.

I felt no wish to spend anything on my body I should spend on others, all what I get. The welfare of others became formost. I prayed to God to keep lit the fire of the desire of redeeming the grifs of others.

The moods keep changing like that of a child frist simple, just mischievious. Feeling grteatful, tearful, more and more.

All the dreams changed into God thoughts. The care for future vanished. I prayed for devotion and love for all. The knowledge of the world seemed futile, increasing ego only. The self-superiority will lead to separation. So there should be no boast of knowlede at all. The life is not for the self. It is for God's mission.

I saw three women sitting on the ox. I approached them and paid my compliments. Somebody introduced them to me as parvati, Laxmi and Sarswati. An inspiration came to me that they should inter my body.

21.8.1989 Swami Ramanand and Satyanand both stood before me.

Many coronets appeared before me. One was placed on my head, others were given to me. I said as to what I would do of them. I was told to give them to others.

I found Swamiji giving me water in a Jug. I placed a plate before him and washed his feet. I took that water and drank. I sang a song to the effect that the Guru was dearer than the prana. I saw 'Ram' word sparkling in the sky. I saw, Bhagwan Shanker was wandering the Kali paltan temple in Meerut. He said that he was waiting for me. He started dancing tandava dance. Parwati laughed and said that Shanker has to dance for the bhaktas.

I pray to Guruji, to visit my heart. The same prayer was repeated by Satyanand and Ram Krishna Parmhanasa. Gurudev placed a coronet on my head at last.

Sometimes a feeling comes that I should renounce everything for the sake of God. But some inner power does not approve it. This conflict goes on occasionally.

On 16.5.1989 during the Jap, the body started revolving and I could not stop it. After sometime all went dark and peaceful. Again, there was a bright light with changing colours. On 17.5.1989 also the body started swinging forward and backward and I stood in Shirshasana pose. The inner voice said that it was due to some internal deficiency. I felt on another occasion that the hands have electric power and if I placed my hand resolutely on some one's body, he would be cured of the ills completely. Different gestures were formed through the fingers at the time of praying to Guru or at the time of singing hymns. These gestures took place involuntarily and without caring for the remarks of others.

I have developed an extreme desire for visiting Digoli. May the Guru grant me an opportunity of that. I have also developed dislike for this pretentious life of the world. I wish to go far off where there should be none but God.

I drifted into sleep, remembering Swamiji. My consciousness disappeared some where. I found myself standing on a high seat made of flowers, and Swamiji standing before me. I told Swamiji that I could not meditate. He asked me to try. I had a vision of indescent picture. I started weeping on looking at it, after sometime, the picture disappeared. I returned to my normal consciousness.

13.6.1989 everything seems changed, inside and outside both. I feel like doing nothing. All is being done by the Mother. She makes me laugh and weep. There is inner happiness as if all the desire was being fulfilled. I realesed that greater the urge, better the fulfillment.

After all, I reached Digoli. The atmosphere proved very helpful. The urge became stronger and stronger. I saw Durga sitting on the back of the lion. She made me sit with her. She disappeared and the lion transformed into a horse. The trident came to me, but I requested Her to keep it with Her.

Shri Virendra Kumar Agrawal

Born in 1936, at Aliganj, Etah district, and educated at Gurukul Vrindaban Shri Virendra Kumar is a cloth dealer at Farrukhabad. His experiences after being initiated at Sadhana dham, kankal, are as follows:

I partook in a Sadhana Dhan camp in 1986, at the inspiration of Parikji. With the atmosphere and the communication of Sadhaks there my Sanskars got awakened. A divine feeling touched me. I got initiated by the inner call. 'Ram Nam' flew into my heart forcefully.

During meditation I found a hand of blessing placed on my head. I bowed reverently to it. I heard a voice saying from within that I could not misuse the power given by me lest it should be withdrawn.

The next day I found white clad, goddess Sarswati standing before me as if to bless. I was enraptured to see this sight. Eyes were swelled with tears. I bowed heartily many times. I felt as if she has come upon my speech.

'Ram Nam' Jap started by itself. The view of life changed completely. I began to think.

गई सो गई, अब राख रही को

"Let past be past; save the rest".

Once I had the vision of Swami Ram during meditation. It seemed he has accepted me as his disciple. My coming to Sadhana Dham became fruitful. Only god-discussion pleased me. I feel intoxicated with spirituality.

After returning home I thought of studying religious books thoroughly. Every action should be done keeping in view the pure life. I took up the study of Geeta, upanished and other religious books by going to the houses of Scholars. A desire of learning Sanskrit also arose. I wished to serve the country through the programmes and actions of Bharat Vikas Parished. I had some chance to speak at the meeting and the people were surprised at that. My internal and external started changing. Regular Jap and Study started. I felt like having wings to aspire to the Sky.

Regular Satsang, started at home for one hour daily.

The reading of religious literature became a routine. It is still continuing. A great change has taken place in my temperament. Though much time can not be devoted due to my business activities but I am confident that the seed sown once has sprouted. On a certain day, it will bear fruit.

Swami Parmanand (Surendra Pal Singh)

Swami Parmanand was born in 1954 at Brindvan and passed Technical Intermediate Examination. He sought initiation at Shripad Baba Brijkala, Academy, Brindavan. He worked in Maintenance Steel Foundry, C.7 F.P., BHEL, Haridwar. He narrates his experiences as follows:

"My initiation towards spirituality was from my boyhood, but a transformation took place only by the grace of the Goodess Jagdamba after I was possessed by her. She removed the miseries of her devotees through this medium. My initiation by Shripad Baba, was also the result of her grace. The opportunity of reading the books 'Anubhut iyon Ke Path Par', also was provided by her. The experiences described in the book seemed to be mine own. I visited Pareekji at Sadhana Dham and listened to his sweet discourses. After hearing my experiences, he took me into the Hall. My gaze was instantly fixed on the picture of Swamiji, as if I were called there by him. This event took place in 1994. After this my visits to Sadhana Dham became regurlar.

One day I was sitting in the room of Dr. Pushpa at Sadhana Dham. She wanted to ask some questions form jagdamba. Immediately I felt possessed by the spirit of Swamiji and I answered all the questions. After this, as I want to enter the prayer room, I found Swamiji standing there to welcome me. I felt dwarfed under his grace. Gurudev gave me 'Ram Nam' mantra, by repeating it three times himself. He also permitted me to deliver it to any one. He resolved all my doubts also. On the advice of Pareekji, I started writing my experiences and here they are:

On the evening of 21.10.1998, I sat for meditation in the Hall. After sometime my breathing became faster like that of the furnace. My nave contracted towards the back, and the arms also contracted inwards. Swamiji stood up before I saw flame rising up from the fireplace. He advised me to practice at home, but never after meal. The interaction lasted 25 minutes. Later Pareek Ji explained that these interactions related to three bandhas i.e. Mool, Udyan and Jalandhar.

On 23.10.1998 I had a possession of Mother. A cry of सी ई

came forth from my mouth. The breathing became heavy and the three bandhas occured. The mouth opened wide, and the tongue watered. The whole body was electrified. Mooladhar and Jalandhar bandhas continued. The neck thrust backward. I felt joy. Soon after my Jaw, widened and the tongue turned towards the palate. The point where the tongue touched seemed to be the mouth of some cave.

The tongue seemed to enter it. After sometime the neck came into natural posture but the body started bending forward. The forehead touched the ground. I was ordered to place the head into the lap and to take the hands backward. I did so and I meditated in this posture. Some voice asked me asto what I wished. I stated that I only wanted to have the Darshan of Bholenath. I had a faint vision which was followed by the vision of Goddess sitting on a lion. I asked nothing but that I should always serve the people. She promised and blessed me that I shall be great Yogi. I shall get Sidhis also. I was made to call my wife. Mother Goddess, applied sindoor in her hair and blessed her to be ever Saubhagyawati.

26.11.1994 Yesterday, I was advised to meditate on heart. I started doing so. I saw a Tapaswi sitting in the lotus posture with a lean body, placing both his hands on the kness. I wanted him to introduce himself. On this he said that he would do, sometime after and disappeared. I used to have vision, of Mother, Gurudev and other divine persons as well.

4.12.1994 I Went to Sadhana Dham, had the vision of Swamiji. All the three bandhas occured. There was streching upward. The neck stiffened, Shivered and became normal again. The Anahat Nad was also audible. Some power seemed to enter through the neck toward the head. After sometimes I felt a jolt, then became normal.

11.12.1994 While sitting in meditation, with all the three Bandhas on, I had the vision of Gurudev Shripad Baba, followed by the vision of Shiva in white complexion. The form changed into that of Kali. The breasts of Shripad baba developed and I sucked their milk. This produced a state of great rapture.

On 16.12.1994 I went to Sadhana Dham to attend a camp. While sitting in the room of Pareekji I had felt possessed by Swamiji's spirit and he welcomed me to the camp. Later I saw Jagdamba standing with a trident in her hand. In the middle of the room. there stood Shivalinga. I saw Brahmaji inside the Pindi. His face began to glow. The figure of Ravana also was there. But the divine voice said that it had the light equal to that of thousands of suns. I worshiped the linga. The eight armed Jagdamba started dancing. The Ram Krishna appeared and advised to continue Sadhana in this very way.

17.12.1994 I Started Meditation in the room of Swamiji where Ramayan and Gurugrantha Sahib were placed on a takhat. I entered meditation. I prostrated at the feet of God and did not give up their touch. A voice said that I shall have to forsake family life. I promised to think over. The voice again asked me to change my name to PARMANAND. I told guruji that I had taken his ASANA. He felt pleased and said that he wanted Yogis like me to go there. I had the vision of NANAK also. I expressed my regret for not continuing the Jap of the mantra given by him. He said that this mantra also was his.

19.12.1994. I sat for meditation. I found that there was a temple with the image of Kali. She held two plates with lit lamps. She entered my body and I felt like her. I expressed the desire to have the Darshan of Shivji. I found that I flew over to a mountain and on the peak of which Shivji was standing. As I went near him, my body became half man and half woman. I thanked Guruji for this kind experience.

Now a days, the method of meditation has changed. Just after sitting the head stretches up and the neck goes underneath. I hear the sound eternal and see the light divine. I feel as if I were being prepared for some celebrated journey. I advise the Sadhaks to leave themselves to the care to Mother. She shall do all good and guide. Let all the wishes of the Sadhaks be fulfilled. Jai Gurudev, Jai Sri Ram.

Rishi Deva Sharma

Born 1952, village Maneda (Bijnor). Passed Intermediate Examination. Place of work BHEL, Ranipur (Haridwar) pressently residing at Jwalapur (Haridwar).

"I had an inclination towards spiritual persuit since boyhood. After reading the book 'Anubhutiyon Ke Path Par, I wished to meet the author of the book. I reached Sadhana Dham on 20.10.1994 with my friend Surendra Pal Singh and met Pareekji. He advised and prompted me to go on the path of Sadhana. I took to his words and started visiting the Dham in the evening and sitting for Jap. I requested Pareekji for Shakti Pat. One day, I was doing Jap, in the prayer room. Suddenly, I felt a movement into my forehead. The Agya Chakra became active. The whole body seemed to rotate. It shivered and I took many rounds, sitting, of course. The women, sitting around felt penickly. Dr. Pushpa advised them to keep silence.

Once while sitting in meditation, my left leg started shaking, followed by the right one. The breath became fast. Later I was told that it was BHASRIKA PRANAYAM, a sure sign of the Kundalini awakening. The breath continued like the furnace. The hands and the feet made many strange gestures. The two legs spread apart and started shaking violently. The neck had twists. The head droped down to touch the ground. These kriyas continued for sometime, regularly.

The other day, I was sitting with Surendra Pal Singh, busy in 'Ram Nam' Jap. I had BHASRIKA started. The hands clapped and the feet fluttered. All these kriyas were being done involuntarily by some unknow power. I used to sit in the last row near the wall, so as to avoid any disturbance. I always depended on the Jap of 'Ram Nam'. All these meditations were looked upon by me with gratitude and faith. I told Parikji every thing and he explained their nature and purpose. He read out portions from books to convince me about these experiences.

One day I woke up 2.30. I started meditating in the bad itself. My body started shaking and breath also became faster. I feel as if I was impelled by some magnetic power. In the darkness, during meditation, different kinds of lights appeared. The lights appeared so charming as to hold the eyes for ever. I saw a rain-bow also once in meditation".

Formerly I knew nothing about Anahat Naad. Now it occurred all the twenty four hours. The whole space seemed vibrant with it. Perhaps this is the real divine music. I heard sometime, the sound of the cricket, or the balls of gongs and JHANJS like those played at the time of Arti in the Temples. I think that the Anahat Naad and lights are the solid examples of the existance of God. Communication with them is communication with God. It was not any exaggeration to say that through these sounds I realised God. These two experiences are Sat, Chit and Anand. They are without beginning and without an end. They are universal and eternal attributes of God. I felt fortunate enough to have all these experiences.

24.10.1994. The whole body started shaking. The hands made different MUDRAS, The internal Kumbhak started and the breath subsided. These interactions continued to take place often.

Many times the anus was compressed with the aid of the pawback. The Apan Vayu, rose up and the stomach stuck to the spine. This posture gave feeling of ecstasy. It is asid that the Nadis and air are purified with this kriya. Digestion improves and the mind becomes peaceful. This is called Uddiyan Bandh. After these two, the Jalandhar band also occurs. When all the three bandhas are on the meditation becomes deep. The desire of remaining in the same posture always develops. Once the head turned down on the hands and the lags went up. I had never tried this SHIRSHASANA. So many asanas which I never had, occurred, effortlessly and occasionally.

When the three bandhas take place and the tongue touches the palate, a state of thought lessness occurs and I desire to enjoy that very state continuously. With the influence of Sadhana Dham and that of Guruji I came to experience so many ASANAS and PRANAYAMS. I do not know what stars favoured me that I was directed to come here.

The very name of Yog frightened one. But this kind of 'Yog' causes no fear because the Guru himself arranges all the Asanas, Pranayams and Mudras. He explains the secrets and the purposes as well. The Sadhak understands everything within himself with the grace of the Guru. The basis of all this is God. His name and faith and submission with this, the Sadhak attains self realisation and blessings eternal.

Raja Ram Misra, 'Shyamraj'
Acharya Shyam Dhyan Kendra

Prof. Raja Ram Misra, the English Translator of this work, was born in Farrukhabad District on Kartika Purnima, Sambat 1982. He inherited spiritual Sanshars from his father. He served for about 37 years and ratired as Head of English Dept. of a College in 1985. Since then, he has been running a Dhyan Kendra and teaching Dhyan to Sadhaks. He is a writer of novels and poetry of repute. His experiences in the field of Sadhana resemble those of other Sadhaks. They are being reproduced below in his own language.

"I was keenly interested in religious and Yogic stuay out believed little in the experiences of the Sadhaks, enumerated in different books. Slowly, I developed an urge for having some spiritual guide. Strangely enough I got a letter on 14th January, 1994 from a famous Yogi. The day was Makar Sankranti. I immediately felt that here was the guide sought and prayed after. I went through the complete literature of Swami Ramanand and felt fully convinced with his views. I started meditating under the guidance of Yog, Shrimani Swami Shyam. I was blessed by Jai Narain Parik also, who was well known to me since the days of my father. I had also the fortune of having the blessings of Pt. Tirjugi Narain Dixit a celebrated Yogi of this district and who was sometime my teacher also. All these associations became possile under some divine scheme to lead me to the true path of realisation.

After meditating for sometime at the space, during the Nav Ratri of 1987, I suddenly heard a very loud noise in the sky. This startled me and though I was sitting in meditation, I felt an electrical sensation throughout my body. A bright circle of light appeared and started rotating on its exis for same moments. I was thrilled as it was the first experience in this field. My body started shaking. The breathing increased too violently. I prayed to Durga Mother to pacify and restore me to the normal condition. I became normal after sometime. I wrote of this experience to my guide and he advised me to proceed on without fear. I started experiencing different colours during meditation. By and by, they disappeared and now only the 'Shyam' sapce remaind.

Now I felt that my guide sat beside me and corrected my postures as and when needed. He expressed his satisfaction. and gave encouragement cons tantly not only in meditation, but during some physical activities like taking bath etc. my guide appeared and masseged and clearnsed my body. A lot of dirt came out of my body. My stool became scanty and body very light and agile. After some months' cleansing process, the kinds of experiences increased. Since under our system of meditation, I had to meditate on space by focussing my attention on an imagenary star, I felt that this star became energised, sometimes it circled very brightly and sometimes threw a focus of divine light on my person. I found myself entering a long long turnnel, leading to immensity. Sometimes delighted and sometimes scared. I tried to procced on.

After some months some physical interactions also started taking place. The three 'bandhas' occurred automatically. I had theoretical knowledge of these asanas, bandhas and chakras, so it was very delightful experience. I meditated twice every day and all the world seemed very gay and grand to me. I devoted to the study of Yogic literature deeply. During all meditation sessions, I had these Kriyas. Though there was ant like sensations in the body, the breath also became heavy but there was lightness in the body often. I had visions of deities, and Sidhas and they seemed to give instructions also. Whenever, I had some doubt, I remembered my guide. He gave instructions and provided explanations in the meditation. The strange thing was that those instructions and explanations were received by me in the letter, from my guide. Later on, when I met my guide personally, I inquired about the systems. He laughed and said that it was all the working of Lord 'Chetan' and the guide and the disciple are never separate. This help from the guide and the experiences of the meditation, made me eager for getting initiated lest something untoward should happen.

I received a call from my guide after I had completed two years of Sadhana. I proceeded to Kullu with some three others Sadhaks. My Guru was waiting for me. He welcomed us. We waited for the initiation but darved not speak to him. On the day our proposed return, we felt very uneasy and disheartened because the purpose for which I had gone, was not being fulfilled. Mysterially enough, we two were called by Swamiji to the pyramid where Swamiji meditated. As we two entered the pyramid, I felt a strange feeling of peace descending upon me. Swamiji bade us sit beside him. He spoke to us for sometings and then asked us to close our eyes and to meditate. After a while, I felt a touch on my head. It was a very gentle but very chilly touch of the fingers of my revered guide. I was thrilled with the touch. The whole body became energised electrically. A current of divine ecstasy ran into the whole body. Soon I went into deep unconscious state and I could not know what happened later on. After sometime, I was asked by the Swamiji to open the eyes and to stand up. I tried my best to do so, but found unable. The whole body was trembling as if in a trance. Violent turmoil was felt in the Stomach. Swamiji laughed and said that there was nothing to worry. All will be well by the evening. What happened to me, was repeated with my other companions also. Later on we discussed and found that our experiences were similar, for almost the whole day. My condition remained static. I ate nothing, we were to leave Kullu on the same evening at 10 PM and as I was unwell my compaions advised for some medical treatment. But Swamiji assured that I shall be perfectly well by the time of departure. I really got well and fit to travel as per schedule. The secret behind all this was the 'Shaktipat' caused by Swamiji on me.

It was an act of his great kindness to me. He moulded my life and thinking with his blessings. I came back to Farrukhabad and activised system of Dhyan Kendra, which is still serving the Sadhaks. In the meantime I have visited my guide regularly once or twice yearly. He has continuously asked and encouraged me to spread the message of Yog. I also feel that most of the people are ignorant about the efficacy of Yog. Great Yogis like Jai Narain Pareek are zealously guiding new Sadhaks.

The Sadhana has now confirmed my faith and the humble exdperiences have convinced that everything can be achieved through Yog and Dhyan. The knowledge of Patanjali Yog Darshan must be assiduously practised by the Sadhak to achieve self-realization. The system may be different but the goal is the same. 'Bagwati Chetna' is the source of all existence and this 'chetna' pervades the whole space. Meditating upon this space brings 'Ritambhara Pragya', ultimately. The experiences of various kinds neither terrify nor surprise any more. They are intimate now. For success in Sadhana submission to God, 'Ishwar Pranidhan' is very necessary. It may be any from or system of Upasana or Dhyan. 'Bhagwati Chetna' in various forms of Shaktis, Gods deities, Rishis, Sidhas and Spiritual Guides, helps the Sadhaks who have pure 'Sanskaras'. All the doubts and suspicions vanish with their blessings. I have been fortunate to realise this, in a very modest way.

One should proceed on the path, with perfect determination, faith and devotion, under the guidence of a real spiritual guide and there shall be no harm or obstacle of any kind. Meditation, creates power enough for me to live well and enjoy the blessings of life. Interactions may come and odds may try to bar the way, but the benevolent power will clear all. It is not possible to relate all the experiences here, as they are various and numerous. Different Sadhaks have experiences occording to their Sadhana. One must only stand assured that his sincers efforts will succeed one day.

Memoirs of my Experiences

Swami Ramanand Visited Farrukhabad in 1943, for the second time. Due to my previous Sanskaras, I came into his contact and this contact grew closer and closer whenever, he visited Farrukhabad. I participated in his Jap, Dhyan and Discussions. But I got the opportunity of being initiated in 1949.

One day, when he sat with the internal Sadhaks, he said, "Some people invite me and I do not feel like accepting it. But there are some from whom I wish to seek something" Saying so, he pointed towards me. I was thrilled to hear this. The next day, he made my home sacred with the dust of his feet. After some refreshment, he started his discourse. The veil of hesitation was now off and we could talk intimately.

One day I expressed my desire to talk to him in private. On being permitted, I approached him with a number of questions. He was sitting on a 'Takhat' in his room. I bowed and sat peacefully at some distance. As soon as I sat, I went into meditation and all the questions disappeared. Half an hour passed when I heard the sound of 'Ram Nam' uttered by him. I got consciousness. Swamiji came to me and pronouncing 'Ram Nam' placed his hand on my head. The whole body felt electrified and my meditation became deeper. I opened my eyes and prostrated at his feet. This was my sudden initiation.

Swamiji went to Nainital and I was permitted to accompany. I remained with him for sometime. I accompanied him again to Ranikhet and then to the camp at Syahidevi. The Charm and the divine grandure affected me deeply. Just at sitting, the 'Chitta Vrittis' subsided and deep meditation could become possible easily.

Different kinds of experiences started taking place. I took down into writing and some of them are as under:–

20.6.1949. I was sitting in commnity upasana at Syahidevi camp (Almora). For some time ideas came and went I sitting cross legged and 'Ram Nam' Jap was proceeding gradually all the thoughts and resolves dis-appeared and, if at all there came any, it was weak and ineffective. Internal grasp increased. After sometime an electric like sensation started in the fingers. Breathing increased. The spine became straight. The whole body felt electrified. Fearlessly, I started expressing my gratitude towards the 'Mahashakti'. I said, "Mother, Let the wish be fulfilled".A period of one and half hour elapsed in all this. All the Sadhaks had gone. I was left alone. Swamiji came and stroked my back affectiontely. I sat as such. He went away but there was no change in my condition. My consciousness turned inwords. Half an hour after Swamiji came again. he wished that I should go into the room. **I had outer consciousness as well.** I could not give up this state nor I had the strength to do so. I said slowly to Swamiji, not to worry and I would go through all. The breath became peaceful gradually. I felt that my body had grown enormous and is going just to touch the roof. I was sitting in the room. I started repeating the mantra तमसो मा ज्योर्तिगमय By and by, I returned to my normal self. But the intoxication was still there. I went into the room of Swamiji and placed my head at his feet. The next day I accompanied Swamiji in his walk. On the way he said that the onset of the force was very deep yesterday. He also said that the burden that I had carried from home, had been cast away. The face itself has changed. After the 'Shaktipat', no evil could enter my body. If it came at all, it shall burn down. He also asserted that I had become free from fear completely. He admitted that after seeing me, he had desired me to join his path and said: But when you did not desire, I could do nothing.

23.6.1949. Yesterday too, I had similar 'kriyas' which I went through gladly and thankfully. Even today, I went into meditation soon after starting the Jap, in the evening I sat crosslegged. The fingers of the hands were intertwined and placed in the lap. After sometime, I sat erect. The neck came into position after some movements. A creaping sensation started in the hands which spread slowly into the whole body. The breathing became faster. The electrical force increased so much that it became rather difficult to sustain. The Jap continued with the intermittant pronouncements of तमसो मा ज्योर्तिगमय and the mantra सर्व मंगल मांगल्ये शिवे सर्वार्थ साधिके. It seemed that some power was making me recite these 'mantras'. As the power force increased, the speed of the chanting of the 'mantras' also increased. During this interaction, the breath was very fast, a sign of Bhasrika pranayam. Even though I was sitting cross legged, the thighs throbbed violently and dashed aginst the earth. I had no fear, instead the heart felt joyous. My urges were being fulfilled thus.

I felt that a flame of fire came out of my nave and enwrapped the whole body. I sat in the midst of it like PRAHLAD sitting in the lap of Holika. I enjoyed the bliss and expressed my gratitude towards my Gurudeva and the 'Mahashakti'. All the Sadhaks had gone. Food was being served. The clank of the plates and the voices were being heard by me. Though left alone, I could not have the strength to get up. It was beyond my power. I was tied with the force of the Divine Power. After two hours, I turned to normality and peace. I recited some two or three Hindi Poems devotionally and I became peaceful then fully.

While I was sitting in the lap of the 'Mahashakti', Swamiji said to the people that I would have been a Hathyogi in the previous life. The obstracted flow has come out suddenly and forcefully.

Most of my 'Malas' and 'VIKARAS', have been expelled thus. I came and placed my head at the feet of Swamiji. He said that it would not occur now so vigorously. It will become normal soon. The influence of the force becomes faster, with the opening of the 'Kendras'. Swamiji, advised me to take light food in the evening. It will facilitate in the Jap and Dhyan in the morning. "Apply sufficient oil to the head. Do not try to be obstinate on your own accord'".

The next day, at the time of the usual walk, Swamiji told me that my mental disorderes have been cured due to the opening of the 'Mooladhar'. It was better that the heap of 'Mal' had flushed out. The Jap would now go, uninterrupted. It was not known when the 'Mooladhar' had opened formerly. It was closed anyhow. This caused hinderance by the external force. It would not happen any more. Remember God. Continue the Jap of 'Ram Nam'. My rememberance will also keep you safe from external forces.

Regarding the Bhasrika Pranayam on the first day, Swamiji said that I should not be afraid of it. After this, the breath becomes quite slow. The breath repeated even minutes after or several minutes after. There was nothing to fear before God. The worst was the death and there was nothing to fear in death. If it comes in the path of seeking God, it is an advantage.

Swamiji gave many pieces of advice at different occasions. Applying oil to the hair, and walking in the open was extremely necessary. It is beneficial to sit by the lamp, lit infront. He told that he had to cry a lot and felt very uneasy in the beginning of his Sadhana. Now it is not so. At the time of prayer and the ARATI, many strange 'Devas' appear but he kept engrossed in himself. These 'Devas' and

'Sidhas' try to help and guide the aspirants.

24.6.1949. I went out for a walk after the communion at about three or four. I ascended the top of a hill. Yonder was the beautiful snow clad Himalyan mountain ranges. I gazed at that. I sat down and spent there two hours in chanting 'OM Namah Shivay'. when I came back, it was the time for evening JAP.

Washing my hands and feet, I sat for prayer. After sometime, the thoughts vanished and I went into Dhyan. A sprout of light felt on my head and the whole body got soaked in it. I became light myself in and out. I saw a beautiful garden, spreading from down to up various kinds of flowers bloomed in it. Trees also appeared in great numbers. I went on seeing all this scene. The midele point of the forehead fluttered beyond description. The whole body was radiant with electrical waves. 'Ram-Nam' Jap continued. I meditated upon तमसो मा ज्योर्तिगमय, मृत्योर्माऽमृतंगमय and I felt tied to some innerpole.

Sometimes, the body seemed very large and the othertime it changed into that of a boy. Tonight, I sat continuously in one posture from 7 to 10.30 when I stood I felt as if my head was going to dash against the roof. I could not keep standing, so sat down again. I chanted 'Ram Nam' and bowed my head to touch the earth repeating ऊ शान्ति, शान्ति, शान्तिः Afterwards, Swamiji, came to me, touched me, and then only I felt that my thaghs were weightless. The body was light like the spurned cotton. I heard the 'NAD' constantly. I went to bed, intoxicated, without taking any food.

I accompanied Swamiji usually during his walks. He explained that the TANTRA Shastras follow the method of energizing Chakras, quite different from ours. The Chakras in our system, awakened automatically and without any danger or harm. He also told that he had seen the Bhasriks Pranayam occuring in others also. It is good that cleansing has been done. Now the Shakti will ascend. I should go on doing my work. He shall help me in need. Taking a Walk in the open is very necessary.

I stayed with Swamiji for one month. Daily various interactions took place at the time of meditation. All the ASANAS occured by themselves. Pranayam Mundras, the ascending of power and the vibration of the Chakras took place. I experienced the visits to other LOKAS. I saw the visions of Sidhas and Devas.

My coming to Swamiji proved blissful. My attitude towards life, completely changed. I visited Syahi Devi Camp again in 1950 and remained with Swamiji for about 15 days. I read my experiences to him. He encouraged and blessed me amply. After returning home, due to irregular sittings and unbalanced food habits, my development stoped. I developed some disorder in the stomach and I had to live on 'COW-MATHA' (butter-milk) for two months completely. I was cured after a long treatment. The path of Sadhana requires, SANYAM, NIYAM (abstenance, ordrliness & DEVOTION).

There would have been untold obstacles in the path of Sadhana, had not the favourable atmosphere of Dava prayag bean available. I came back home in 1953 due to my illness. I lay in my room day and night. After the improvement in my health the Yogic 'Kriyas' started again and continued for about a month and half. The 'Kriyas' are so numerous that they can not be described here fully.

It seemed as if Ram Krishna were getting all these Kriyas performed under his guidance. I had carefully gone through his books 'Ram Krishna Vachnamrite' and Ram Krishna Leelamrita". Their study also seemed to influence. The Kriyas started after the performer once ended. Guru Ramanand appeared, usually and the visions of Sidhas and Devas were also there. The 'Kriyas' continued for the full night sometimes. Often I performed these Kriyas in a quite naked form. My wife cooperated fully in this matter.

Once, due to my weak body, I could not sustain the force of the SHAKTI. All the members of the family became worried. I thought it proper to give a break to the Sadhana. I prayed and all the Bundhas, seemed to loose throughout the night. At down and day break a Black Serpent seemed to come out of my nose. It went towards the sun and I returned to my normal position. While watching the Sun I had feeling that it is the source of all beings. The life giving consciousness entered my body and I became completely fearless.

By and by, I became normal. Since then Ram Nam Jap and listening to the Anahat Naad, have become a part of my nature. Not I, but they have possessed me. I repeat to my companions.

आंखें मूद कर सुनिए सितार, राम नाम मधुर झंकार।
इसमें मन का मेल मिलाओ, राम नाम स्वर में ही समाओ।

Now my wish is that my resolve of spiritual fulfilment should be continued through the medium of my dear brothers and sisters. Their evolution is mine; their experiences and realizations are mine.

Author

